DON'T THROW FEATHERS AT CHICKENS

A Collection of Texas Political Humor

Charles Herring, Jr.
Walter Richter

Wordware Publishing, I
REGIONAL DIVIS

Published by:
Wordware Publishing, Inc.
1506 Capital Avenue
Plano, Texas 75074

ISBN 1-55622-311-0
10 9 8 7 6 5 4 3 2
9205

All inquiries for volume purchases of this book should be addressed
to Wordware Publishing, Inc., at the above address. Telephone
inquiries may be made by calling:

(214) 423-0090

ACKNOWLEDGMENTS

The authors are extremely grateful for the good humor and wit of countless generations of Texas politicians and officeholders. Without them, this book could not be, and more importantly, state politics and government would be much less fun and probably much less successful human endeavors. Politics and government service are tough and demanding professions, more so now than ever before, and despite all of the politico fun-poking in this volume, we deeply respect and appreciate the dedication and commitment of those who selflessly devoted their lives to these worthy, underappreciated professions. To them we dedicate this volume.

Very special thanks to Governor Ann Richards for her kind and overly generous Foreword to this book. She is a great Governor, a wonderful friend, and unquestionably one of the most talented political humorists in the history of Texas.

We also deeply appreciate the generosity, talent, and political insight of Ben Sargent, the Pulitzer Prize winning political cartoonist of the *Austin American Statesman*, who contributed art for this book.

Molly Ivins, the foremost political humor columnist in Texas, currently a columnist for the *Fort Worth Star Telegram*, and a true Texas treasure, is responsible, either directly or by inspiration, for much of whatever entertainment value the reader finds in this volume. With permission from Molly we have used many items from her own book, *Molly Ivins Can't Say That, Can She?* (Random House, Inc. 1991). Everyone who enjoys political humor should have at least three copies of her book because friends will surely steal at least two of the copies.

Likewise, as shown by the Source Notes at the back of this volume, Texas writer, publisher, and political commentator Sam Kinch, Jr. has made absolutely invaluable contributions to this project. Sam publishes *Texas Weekly* (P.O. Box 5306, Austin, Texas 78763), the preeminent

weekly report on Texas politics and government. Not only is Sam an extraordinarily savvy political analyst, but he also has published in *Texas Weekly* a marvelous collection of anecdotes and "Quotes of the Week," from which we have borrowed extensively. Sam generously devoted his considerable talents and encyclopedic knowledge to reviewing much of the text and catching various errors in esoteric matters of Texas political history that probably no one knows as well as Sam.

We also owe a special debt to Mark McCulloch of CheckMark Typesetting. Mark provided essential technical advice for our editing and publishing, as well as all-around spiritual enlightenment and support.

Of course, we owe our most special thanks to our infinitely supportive spouses, Ginny Agnew and Dorothy Jean Richter, for their political commitment, inspiration, and abiding humor and warmth — but mostly just for putting up with us.

Last, but certainly not least, many friends and leaders have gone above and beyond the call of duty in helping us with this collection, and we owe particular thanks to Senator Lloyd Bentsen, Lieutenant Governor Bob Bullock, Railroad Commissioner Lena Guerrero, Congressman Jake Pickle, State Senator Carl Parker, Liz Carpenter, Bob Armstrong, Cactus Pryor, Arthur Gochman, Arnold Garcia, and Sam Attlesey.

Charles Herring, Jr.

Walter Richter

TABLE OF CONTENTS

Don't Throw Feathers at Chickens

This is an old country saying which may have originated in West Texas. It roughly means, "Don't give people something they already have, give 'em something new." For political purposes, the saying could be translated as "Don't tell the people what they already know, tell 'em what they want to hear."

FOREWORD

I once talked to a leading member of Congress about a piece of legislation that I wanted passed.

He waxed philosophical about its chances but said that one group of congressmen was giving him a very difficult time with their opposition to some parts of the complex piece of legislation. I ventured the opinion that his opponents were only trying to have their voices be heard on the subject and that they would go along with the bill eventually.

"Have their voices be heard?" thundered the member, a crusty old committee chairman. "Don't they know that the best way to have your voice heard in Congress is to sit down and shut up?"

Probably good advice, but advice that politicians are hard pressed to follow.

Taking such advice also would be tragic because politicians wouldn't have nearly the opportunity to say and do the foolish things that make such great political stories.

And then we wouldn't be blessed with the delightful anecdotes and *bons mots* compiled in this volume.

Chuck Herring and Walter Richter have collected classic examples of Texas political humor, wit, and wisdom, and everyone who enjoys either humor or politics will enjoy this book.

I am indebted to them for putting all of this in one place. It makes stealing speech material so much easier!

And they even have an index. Very thoughtful.

Governor Ann Richards
Austin, Texas

PREFACE

"There are three things that are real: God, human folly, and laughter. The first two are beyond comprehension. So we must do what we can with the third."

John F. Kennedy

The authors are Democrats.

That's probably the best thing we can say about ourselves. Some of our friends would say that's the only good thing we can say about ourselves. With much less accuracy, we refer to ourselves as authors of this volume. The real authors, of course, are the countless candidates, office-holders, and commentators whose speeches and quips we've heard and read over the years. Ann Richards, Lyndon Johnson, Bob Bullock, Jim Hightower, and dozens of other superb political humorists who have run for and held office in Texas have written this book. We have simply listened, read, and compiled, and occasionally edited.

Between us, we have actively campaigned for Democrats for 82 years; and we've served four terms as Travis County Democratic Party Chairs, which by itself is reason enough to doubt our sanity and judgment.1 We've enjoyed that collective experience immensely — mostly — and we've enjoyed listening to hundreds of wonderful political speeches.

Texas has been blessed with a rich, mixed tradition of great political humor and, sometimes at least, egregiously bad government that has been easy to poke fun at. With

---

1   How do you find a County Chair? Longtime Travis County Democratic Chair Bob Sneed had this stock advice: You simply approach just about any local citizen and inquire, "Could you direct me to the village idiot?"

Ann Richards as Governor, the humor is better than ever and so is the government.

In his superb collection of national political humor, *Too Funny To Be President*, Mo Udall aptly observed that humor is the "best antidote for the politician's occupational disease: an inflated, overweening, suffocating sense of self-importance."

Udall points out that one of President James Garfield's aides advised him "never make the people laugh; to succeed you must be solemn, solemn as an ass." Garfield obeyed, was elected, and three months later someone shot him. Calvin Coolidge concurred in the same theory, but not the practice: "I think the American public wants a solemn ass as president . . . and I think I'll go along with them." Fortunately, legions of Texas politicians have rejected such "asininity."

Political speeches and discourse are public. That leads us to what is perhaps an obvious caution: aficionados of Texas political humor will have heard many of the stories in this volume before, sometimes many times before, and often told by or attributed to other politicians, authors, or storytellers. Mark Shields says that political jokes have a copyright of "about twelve hours," and Columnist Art Buchwald follows this rule: "The first two times you use a joke, give your source credit. From then on, to hell with it!" We've included notes in the back of this volume to identify our sources whenever possible. We compiled this book from our own notes, often originally scribbled on the backs of napkins, from other books, from newspapers, and from many generous officeholders and friends who gave us their favorite items. Our selection criteria were simple: items had to be told or written by or about Texas politicians. We applied even those loose criteria very loosely.

The organizational principles we've followed in this book are similarly loose and meandering. Almost by definition, political humor is brief and anecdotal. Often the same joke or story could logically appear in three different chapters — if we were logical, which we aren't very. As a partial remedy, we've included an index by name, so that you can locate your favorite speakers more easily.

As is obvious from the length, this volume is not comprehensive or all-inclusive, and it's certainly not the final word on Texas political humor. It's just a sampling, a small fraction of the political humor items the authors have collected over the years, and an even smaller fraction of the items we have received from friends and donors. We probably just forgot a lot of stuff, too, but we feel quite comfortable in blaming each other for any such omissions or other errors. As penance, and somewhat optimistically, and probably as much for our own enjoyment as for any other reason, we've already started working on a second volume of material. At the back of this volume we've included instructions on how readers can send in additional material, and we will deeply appreciate all contributions.

"There are three things worth being — a preacher, a teacher, or a politician."
Lyndon B. Johnson

CHAPTER ONE

Introduction(s)

"What I value more than all things
is good humor."

- Thomas Jefferson

How to begin? Every political speaker confronts that question with every speech. Even before the featured speech, however, another speaker usually introduces the real speaker. Sometimes yet another speaker introduces the introducer. The theory seems to be that a speaker cannot say nice things about himself or herself, or else we audience members will conclude — and presumably be shocked — that the speaker has a Big Ego. This polite fiction has complete transparency, but the tradition is ancient and well-nigh inviolable.

The introducer's job, of course, is to praise the speaker to the highest of heavens. Properly given, the introduction leaves the audience confused as to whether it is hearing an introduction or a eulogy, or as is sometimes said, the difference between the typical testimonial type introduction and a eulogy is that, at the testimonial, at least one listener believes what is said.

The fundamental laws of the universe appear to make it impossible to praise the person being introduced so excessively that the person actually disbelieves or is embarrassed by the remarks. Lyndon Johnson implicitly recognized the impossibility of such excess when he responded to a particularly warm introduction this way: "I've known your distinguished president for many years. I am indebted to him for many things, including his wise counsel through the years, his willingness to always serve his country, and for tonight's wonderful laudatory introduction. It seems to me it's one of the best introductions I've ever had. As I think about it, probably this was the best introduction I've ever had except for one other occasion, and that was when I was speaking down in the hills of Tennessee and the governor was supposed to introduce me and he didn't get there in time, so I had to introduce myself."

By custom, the typical and best response to such an introduction is self-deprecating, designed to send the message that "Sure, I'm great, but I can also poke fun at myself, which really means I'm a nice guy, too, which makes me even more wonderful than the introducer said." Thus, Representative Ciro Rodriquez had this winning response to a gracious introduction: "I thank you so much for the kind words. You know, not all introductions are so wonderful. Once I was at a dinner sitting next to a youthful host who was to introduce me, and he asked me what he should say about me by way of introduction. Because the evening's program was behind schedule, I simply told him that the less said about me the better. The host came through alright, and in introducing me he said: 'Our next speaker is Mr. Rodriquez, and the less you say about him, the better.'"

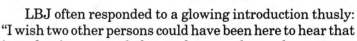

LBJ often responded to a glowing introduction thusly: "I wish two other persons could have been here to hear that introduction — my father and my mother — because my father would have enjoyed it, and my mother would have believed it."

Another favorite self-effacement is adapted to audiences who don't really know the speaker: "I appreciate those kind remarks very much. They were a considerable improvement over an introduction I received on another occasion recently. My introducer began by explaining he had been asked at the last minute to make the introduction. He said, 'Dr. Moore was supposed to introduce our speaker this evening, but he had an emergency call and had to leave. I asked him what to say by way of introduction and he told me all I had to say was that our speaker needs no introduction. I sure hope that's true because I never heard of him before.'"

Senator Richter, with his German name and a Central Texas constituency, often could get away with the following opening remarks after a particularly flowery introduction. "I am reminded of the German-American maid named Hulda who on a given Friday asked for a couple of days off so she could get married. This was granted, but the lady of the house was startled when Hulda on the following Friday asked for a couple more days off the next week.

'What in the world for?' asked the missus.

'I want to see a lawyer about a divorce.'

Puzzled, the lady asked, 'You just got married, and now you want a divorce? What's this all about?'

'Ma'am,' responded Hulda, 'that man was the most over-introduced squarehead I ever saw.'"

Another effective response is to be reminded of the occasion when the legendary Dizzy Dean, who prided himself on being a solid batsman as well as a star pitcher, was batting and reacted sharply to a called strike.

"Are you blind?" he yelled at the umpire. "That ball was a mile high."

Whereupon the ump replied, calmly, "Come off it, Dean, that ball was coming so fast, you didn't even see it."

"Well," grumped Dizzy, "it sure sounded high."

Well, the honored speaker declares, "I liked that introduction a lot, but I did think it sounded a little high."

———— ★ ————

The late John Henry Faulk was not only a national treasure as a champion of free speech, the First Amendment, and human rights generally, he also was a storyteller and after-dinner speaker nonpareil. He liked to include in his opening response to introductions the account of how a "friend" had once introduced him. "I can tell you two things about Johnny. The first is, he has never been in the Texas Penitentiary. The second is, I don't know why."

———— ★ ————

With Texas rural audiences, politicos sometimes give this old-time response to a warm introduction and applause received on a cold day: "I appreciate your welcome. As the cow said to the Amarillo farmer, 'Thank you for a warm hand on a cold morning.'"

———— ★ ————

The most common mistake of political speeches is to go on too long. Audiences love brevity. Regardless of a speaker's absolute certainty that his or her talk or program is fabulously brilliant, ingenious, and unpredecented in human intellectual history, if the talk is too long, it ain't good. At least not for most political audiences. This was less true in the past and in the days before television, when lengthy political orations were an art form, a seasonal entertainment of choice in courthouse squares around the state.

Tragically, TV has shrunk attention spans to microscopic dimensions. What Tom Brokaw of "NBC News" refers to as "the cancer of the sound bite" has reduced the length of the average quote for presidential candidates appearing on TV evening news from forty-three seconds in 1968 to nine seconds in 1988. If that shrinkage rate continued through 1992, sound bites would be 2 seconds. Try expressing an important idea on a critical issue of global import in two seconds.

In fact, consider the classic oration of Brutus in Shakespeare's play *Julius Caesar*, which takes about twenty seconds to say: "Friends, Romans, Countrymen, Lend me your ears; I come to bury Caesar, Not to praise him. The evil that men do lives after them; The good is oft interred with their bones." In two seconds, you can say "Friends, Romans."

The point is that audiences don't like long speeches, and even in times past, brevity was a well-recognized virtue in political rhetoric. Thomas Jefferson said that "speeches measured by the hour die by the hour." Benjamin Franklin gave the same advice, though somewhat more sarcastically: "Here comes the orator, with his flood of words, and his drop of reason."

Abe Lincoln, too, had a famous put-down of a long-winded windbag: "He can compress the most words into the smallest idea of any man I ever met."

In Texas, a political speech is sometimes referred to as a Longhorn: one that makes two good points, but they are a long way apart and have a lot of bull in between.

Ruben Bonilla tells a good version of another opening joke that relates the perils of prattling on too long. "I use this joke in a group with one prominent individual in leadership who has been with the organization for a long time and is held in senior statesman status. I announce that it is not particularly well known but this senior statesman, in his earlier days, was quite a fisherman. He regularly fished the lakes, rivers, and creeks of his home county by himself and brought back enormous volumes of fish.

"The day did come, however, when he invited his brother-in-law, who had only recently married his sister, to go fishing with him. As it happened, his brother-in-law also was the county's newly-appointed game warden.

"They went to a small lake in that county and rowed to the middle. The senior statesman, who had said not a word during the entire trip, reached into his tackle box, pulled out a stick of dynamite, lit it, and threw it into the lake. Boom!! The fish came to the top — dead fish floated everywhere. He scooped up the fish in the net, put them in the bottom of the boat, and said not a word.

"The game warden, his brother-in-law, was shocked. He shouted at his brother-in-law, 'You can't fish that way! I'm telling you! I'm the game warden and I don't care who you are, whether you're kinfolk or not, the next person I see throw a lighted stick of dynamite into this lake, I'm gonna arrest them and put them in jail! You stop that, and you stop that right now!'

"The senior statesman quietly reached back into his tackle box, pulled out another stick of dynamite, lit it, handed it to his brother-in-law the game warden and said, 'You gonna fish, or you gonna talk?'"

———————— ★ ————————

Mo Udall tells a good story about what can happen when the speaker goes on too long. An Agriculture Department bureaucrat was invited to address a cattlemen's association in rural West Texas. In a high-pitched voice, the bureaucrat droned on for two hours. Toward the end of his speech, he noticed that some of the men in the audience were unholstering their guns. After he finished, he nervously eyed the surly men and asked the chairman if he was in danger.

"No, you are our guest, so you are safe. But I wouldn't want to be the program chairman."

Udall also told an LBJ yarn demonstrating the risks of verbosity. "A former senator was speaking down home and he started out talking about the beautiful piney woods of east Texas. Then he moved out onto the plains dappled with bluebonnets and then down through the hill country to the Gulf Coast. The crowd was becoming restless as he continued the rhetorical state tour, going back to the piney woods and droning on about bluebonnets. When he finished his second circuit, he came up for air, but then set off talking once again about the piney woods and the bluebonnets.

"At this, a good old boy rose up in the back of the room and yelled out, 'The next time you pass Lubbock, how about letting me off.'"

The late Congressman Bob Poage told this "hangman's story," one of his personal favorites, to illustrate the virtues of brevity.

"Thank you for the warm applause, ladies and gentlemen. This is the second time I've had the privilege to speak to this wonderful assemblage and I'm quite honored by the opportunity. I know not to repeat myself, however, and that reminds me of the story of a big hanging that occurred long, long ago in my hometown of Waco, Texas. The case having been a sensational one, a great throng gathered to watch the villain get strung up. After placing the noose over the neck of the felon, the hangman announced that in such circumstances the prisoner had the right to make a final statement if he had any last words.

Once, when introducing his vice president Hubert H. Humphrey, Lyndon Johnson said, "All that Hubert needs is a gal to answer the phone and a pencil with an eraser."

"The prisoner responded, 'Nope, I ain't got nuthin' to say.'

"At this point, a fellow in the crowd near the front waved his arms wildly to get the hangman's attention, shouting, 'Sir, I'm a candidate for Congress from this district, and I wonder if the prisoner would yield his time so that I could address this wonderful gathering.'

"The hangman turned to the prisoner: 'You heard what the man said; what is your pleasure?'

"'Shucks,' he answered, 'I got no objection to that. But if you don't mind, please go ahead and hang me first. I've heard him speak before.'"

That story also was a favorite of LBJ, who had other gallows humor. To point out the evils lurking in some ill-conceived piece of proposed legislation, he would sometimes tell this one. "Around the turn of the century there was a fellow who was about to be hanged in Fredericksburg, Texas. As was the custom thereabouts, the sheriff asked the fellow if he'd like to inspect the gallows. The prisoner replied 'Yes, sheriff, I reckon I better do that, if you don't mind.' The sheriff said sure, that was his right, and slowly they walked around the gallows together, with the prisoner inspecting the entire structure quite closely. When they finished the tour, the sheriff asked if the man had anything to say. The prisoner responded in a slow drawl, 'Well, ya know sheriff, I'll be honest with ya. To me the damned thing jes' don't look safe.'"

Dallas financier and political contributor Jess Hay has a more topical gallows story, resulting from the Texas savings and loan industry collapse, which as one wag put it, "has injured quite a few Texas bankers, lawyers, politicians, and even a few innocent citizens." Anyway, Hay asks and answers this question:

"How do you get a banker out of a tree? You cut the rope."

Similarly cheery was S&L owner John Selman's comment about the same predicament: "If you own an S&L in Texas, you sleep like a baby — you wake up every three hours and cry."

Congressman Jake Pickle of Austin is not only one of the most effective congressmen in the state's history, he's a man of limitless energy and good humor. To reassure an audience that his remarks will be brief he sometimes tells a story about a long-winded preacher. One Sunday the preacher was annoyed to see a parishioner walk out before the end of his sermon. When the preacher next encountered the person, he asked why the fellow had walked out, and the reply was that he had left to get a haircut. This answer baffled the preacher, who asked "In heaven's name, if you needed a haircut, why didn't you get one before you came to church?" "Because, reverend," the man explained, "when I came to church, I didn't need a haircut."

———— ★ ————

During the planning of a fund-raiser for the Travis County Democratic Party while Senator Richter was Party Chair, discussion turned to possible speakers, and someone mentioned the name of legendary Travis County Democrat and former U. S. Senator Ralph Yarborough. Several of the "planners" cautioned that our beloved Senator often tended to talk at great length once he got started and that an overly long speech might leave too little time for the scheduled auction. Richter developed this proposal to protect the schedule.

"I went to the Senator's office and told him that we would like for him to address our meeting. He agreed. Then I said, 'Senator, I trust you won't be offended when I tell you that there is some concern that you might talk too long, and I've come up with a suggestion. I wonder if you would mind if in our advertisement of this event we mention that you are going to make a ten-minute talk. We would state further that for every minute over ten that you speak, you have agreed to pay the Travis County Democratic Party $25.' The Senator's eyes twinkled and, without a moment's hesitation, he declared, 'That's a deal! Provided, that is, that the Party will pay me $25 for every minute under ten that I talk.' We both laughed and left it at that. Just for the fun of it, I timed the Senator and he did talk over ten minutes — like about 30 seconds!"

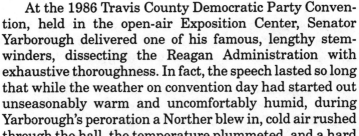

At the 1986 Travis County Democratic Party Convention, held in the open-air Exposition Center, Senator Yarborough delivered one of his famous, lengthy stemwinders, dissecting the Reagan Administration with exhaustive thoroughness. In fact, the speech lasted so long that while the weather on convention day had started out unseasonably warm and uncomfortably humid, during Yarborough's peroration a Norther blew in, cold air rushed through the hall, the temperature plummeted, and a hard rain began to fall. After the speech, one admiring listener concluded: "Yarborough always talks long, but this time he did the impossible. He began talking during the summer, and talked till winter came — and kept the heat on the Republicans the whole time!"

Another long-windedness tale is about the new seminary graduate who was sent to an isolated village in the ranch country to establish a church. Despite the fact that he had tried to spread the word that his first service would be held in one of the town's several vacant buildings, on the appointed morning only one old rancher appeared. After waiting for an extra half hour in the vain hope that others might come, the young man finally asked the old fellow if he should go ahead with the preaching. The grizzled old-timer allowed as how when he took a load of hay out in the pasture to feed his cattle and only one cow showed up, he'd still feed her. Whereupon our young preacher proceeded with the service. It being his first sermon, however, he got carried away and he went on and on and on. When he finally stopped, he rushed over to his lone listener who was wearily getting to his feet. "Well, sir, how did I do?" "I'll tell you," drawled the old fellow, "when I take a load of hay out to the pasture to feed the cows and only one cow shows up, I don't give her the whole load."

Then there's the old no-notes ploy. LBJ would sometimes lead off with this intro: "We had a preacher back home who dropped his notes and his dog grabbed them and tore them up. And when the preacher went into the pulpit he apologized to his congregation and said 'I am very sorry today. I have no sermon. I'll just have to speak as the Lord directs. But I'll try to do better next Sunday.'"

An elected official in an audience may be called on for a statement, without any prior warning. With the proper (i.e., not so proper) audience, one former Texas legislator, now lobbyist, was fond of responding this way: "This reminds me of the time that Marc Antony visited Cleopatra. Opening the door to her boudoir, Marc found her beguilingly draped across a couch, clad only in a flimsy negligee. Spying him, she gushed, 'It's so good to see you, Marc. Come here and whisper sweet nothings in my ear.' Whereupon he replied, 'Look, Cleo, I did not come here to make a speech.'" Here follows a Jack Benny-type pause, and then the second laugh-line: "Cleopatra's coy response was 'Well, Marc my sweet, I'm not prone to argue.'"

And if all else fails, there is the self-inflicted pratfall. Longtime Speaker of the Texas House of Representatives, Gib Lewis, unquestionably has been a highly skilled legislative leader. Even more indisputable, however, is his title as the Texas Master of Malapropism. He is so good at being so bad grammatically, and generally so good-natured about it, that some observers have suspected he is simply a clever practitioner of verbal slapstick, a Charlie Chaplin of the microphone. As we will see below, however, long experience proves otherwise pretty conclusively. Gib doesn't try to be funny, he just is. One of the Gibber's most famous flubs was during a ceremony in the House to honor Texans with disabilities. This was a simple, routine ceremonial proclamation, and Gib read the appropriate resolutions flawlessly. Then, in a faux pas that will live in perpetuity in the annals of Texas political humor, Gib turned to a House gallery packed with disabled citizens in wheelchairs, and said "Will all of you now please stand and be recognized?"

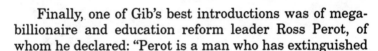

Finally, one of Gib's best introductions was of mega-billionaire and education reform leader Ross Perot, of whom he declared: "Perot is a man who has extinguished himself in many fields."

On that note, we extinguish this chapter.

CHAPTER TWO

Campaign Trail

P olitical campaigns can be hell, and they usually are. That's not surprising. Logistically, campaigns are phenomenal conglomerations. A candidate, a few friends, a few strangers, some consultants, and a fund-raiser or two, try to fabricate a Rube Goldbergian organization, overnight, to deal with large masses of hostile, or at best apathetic, voters, and deal with vicious, cynical media who are blithely ignorant of the issues and seemingly determined to prevent the candidate from communicating with the voters in any meaningful or substantive manner, thus relegating the campaign to a battle of obscenely expensive and preposterously misleading, shallow, and uninformative commercial advertising. Great fun!

Thus, a sense of humor can be a critically important survival tool for the candidate. It makes life on the campaign trail more endurable for the candidate and staff, and it also can make the candidate more attractive to the public.

Why would a rational human being willingly undertake such an insane, masochistic ordeal? In Texas, irrationality and masochism are widespread. Texas Comptroller John Sharp had this description of his own previous decision to run for the Texas Railroad Commission during tough economic times. "They asked me why I ran for the RRC with $10 oil prices. It's like the drunk who was arrested for being drunk, jumping in bed and setting his bed on fire. The drunk replied that he was guilty of intoxication, but the bed was already on fire before he jumped in it."

Like most excruciatingly painful, nearly fatal experiences, campaigning can build character, toughness, and even judgment, at least for those participants who survive the ordeal. Former U. S. Speaker of the House Sam Rayburn expressed this reservation about the brilliant, youthful team that accompanied John Kennedy into the White House: "I'd feel a lot better if just one or two of them had ever run for sheriff."

Cynics identify two kinds of voters: the apathetic and the hostile. One standard definition of democracy is "a form of government by popular ignorance," and another is George Bernard Shaw's: "The system that substitutes election by the incompetent many for appointment by the corrupt few."

Texas appellate judge Ben Z. Grant recounted the difficulties of making an impression on voters even when the candidate figures out a way to attract attention. "I was a delegate to the Constitutional Convention in 1974, and I rode a horse 286 miles from Marshall to the Convention in Austin in an attempt to dramatize the obsoleteness of some of the provisions in the Texas Constitution. The trip took eight and one half days. (I could have gotten the mail contract if I could have made it in five.) I had all my troubles behind me by the time I got to Austin.

"The horse that I rode was named Miss Entertainment, which hardly seemed appropriate for a politician, so I renamed her Miss Liberty in honor of the sixteen-foot lady atop the State Capitol Building. The county judge said that by the time I reached the county line, I would rename her Miss Calculation.

"I was filled with self-importance as I passed a small community school and the children, not even from my own legislative district, came out to the fence shouting, 'Hi, Ben Grant! Hi, Ben Grant!' Here I was more than a hundred miles from home and all these kids knew my name. I began to wonder just how famous a fellow can get in one lifetime. Just before I got out of earshot, a little boy, seven or eight years old, who had been waving and saying 'Bye, Ben Grant! Bye, Ben Grant!' turned to his teacher and asked, 'Teacher, who is that man riding Ben Grant?'"

Attorney General Dan Morales also has a good "kids" story. He had escorted a group of elementary school children around the Capitol for about an hour telling them how state government works. He was particularly impressed with the stack of thank-you notes he received a few days later, one of them from a boy who called Morales the best speaker he'd ever heard, though he also noted that Morales was the only speaker he'd ever heard. Another said he had seen Morales on TV and noted that he "looked fatter in person than on the screen." A third student simply wrote, "I wish we had gone to the zoo."

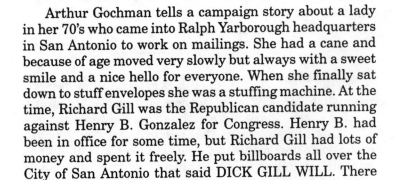

Arthur Gochman tells a campaign story about a lady in her 70's who came into Ralph Yarborough headquarters in San Antonio to work on mailings. She had a cane and because of age moved very slowly but always with a sweet smile and a nice hello for everyone. When she finally sat down to stuff envelopes she was a stuffing machine. At the time, Richard Gill was the Republican candidate running against Henry B. Gonzalez for Congress. Henry B. had been in office for some time, but Richard Gill had lots of money and spent it freely. He put billboards all over the City of San Antonio that said DICK GILL WILL. There were two of those billboards within sight of the Yarborough headquarters. She walked in one day and asked Arthur, "Who is this fellow Gill Will?"

———— ★ ————

An all too common nightmarish reality in Texas is the legitimate candidate who draws an unknown, but well-named opponent. Land Commissioner Garry Mauro, for example, had one race against M. D. Anderson, not M. D. Anderson the excellent Houston hospital, but M. D. Anderson the bartender. The opponent's name was perfect: it was not so well known that everyone would immediately recognize the medical building origin, but it was sufficiently familiar that there was a real danger that a citizen in the voting booth was likely to say "M. D. Anderson, M. D. Anderson, now who is that? Boy, I know that's familiar, but I just can't remember. I know this Anderson fellow has done something real good. Mauro ain't bad, but this Anderson must really be something. I probably ought to vote for him." A nightmare!

———— ★ ————

Voters remain the ultimate danger in any officeholder's life, and thus Wynn Catlin defined democracy as "the art of saying 'nice doggie, nice doggie' until you can find a rock."

———— ★ ————

Perhaps too often, Texas voters get what they deserve, reap what they sew, stew in their own juices, and drown in other cliches that equate with getting the quality or lack of quality of government that is inevitable if not enough good people participate in the system. As the brilliant and scintillating humorist and political commentator Molly Ivins has surveyed the historical results in the governor's office in Texas: "In Texas, we do not hold high expectations from the office; it's mostly been occupied by crooks, dorks and the comatose." Molly chronicled, as only Molly can, a period in which the 1990 Texas Democratic Primary gubernatorial battle deteriorated into a duel of would-be executioners:

> They held a Fry-Off. Mattox got on television and announced he couldn't wait to pull that old death-penalty lever; when he was A.G. he used to go up to the state pen and watch guys get fried for the fun of it. Mark White got on television and actually strolled through a gallery of baddies who'd been fried when he was governor while he talked about how keen he is on frying people. Richards kept saying, "Me too." Mattox found some prison newsletter that had endorsed Richards and put up an ad that said, "Vote for Jim Mattox: *He* hasn't been endorsed by anyone on death row." You'd have thought they were all running for State Executioner. "Saturday Night Live" did a satirical skit on the primary in which the candidates wore black hoods and carried axes.

———————— ★ ————————

Statewide candidacies suffer statewide problems. Former State Senator Tom Creighton — and many others — tell this ancient story of Jim "Pa" Ferguson, the only Texas governor ever to be impeached. Ferguson was on the campaign trail one time seeking the governorship. He got a telephone call from his campaign manager, who was in Dallas. "Jim," he said, "you better get yourself up here to Dallas in a hurry. Your opposition is telling the durn'est pack of lies on you that you can imagine."

Replied Jim: "Dallas, hell! I gotta get to Houston. I got much worse problems down there. My enemies are all over town down there and they're telling the truth on me!"

———— ★ ————

After Pa Ferguson's impeachment, his wife Ma Ferguson ran for governor and ultimately was elected twice. Critics maintained that Pa was actually still running state government from behind the scenes, and apparently his manipulative skills continued to be applied on occasion. The story is told that once Ma was accidentally jostled by a fellow as they were both getting off the elevator on the second floor of the Capitol. The man said, "Oh, pardon me, Governor." Whereupon Ma answered, "Now, you'll have to talk to Jim about that. His office is downstairs." On another occasion Ma Ferguson was confronted with the question of whether children should be punished for speaking Spanish in the public schools of Texas. Ma responded: "If the English language was good enough for Jesus Christ, it is good enough for the children of Texas."

———— ★ ————

Many Texas campaigning politicos have quoted and sympathized with Mark Twain's description of the missionary who set out to convert a tribe of cannibals: "They listened with the greatest of interest to everything that he had to say. Then, they ate him." Similarly, Mo Udall identified the principal difference between a dog and a voter: "It is said that if you find a starving dog, feed him, and make him prosperous, he will not bite you, whereas a voter will."

———— ★ ————

Voters come in all shapes and sizes, and in Texas at least, all stages of life and death. A New Mexico official once ribbed John White about the Governor of Texas (Dolph Briscoe at the time) having appointed a dead man to a commission. Responded White: "If they're eligible to vote, they ought to be eligible to be appointed to a commission."

———— ★ ————

Former U.S. Speaker of the House Jim Wright capsulized the can't-win treatment a congressman often receives at the hands of hometown constituents: "When I returned to my district office there were long and loud complaints that I was spending too much time there and should be in Washington. Then, when I didn't make it for several weeks, others said, 'Who does that guy think he is? We only see him during elections.'"

———— ★ ————

Discretion may be the better part of valor, but as Maury Maverick, Jr. explained to John Kennedy, it simply isn't always possible. During the 1960 presidential campaign, Maury was advance man for the San Antonio trip. At the Alamo, Kennedy gave a rousing speech to ten thousand people. Maverick then gave Kennedy a tour inside. After the tour a Kennedy aide said, "Maury, let's get Jack out the back door to avoid the crowd."

Maverick's response, which got him in some little trouble when it became public: "Hell, there's no back door at the Alamo. That's why we had so many dead heroes."

———— ★ ————

Another Alamo comparison came from journalist and LBJ confidant Liz Carpenter. When party-switching former Governor John Connally said he would head the Richard Nixon campaign in 1972, Liz was moved to say: "It's a good thing John Connally wasn't at the Alamo. He'd be organizing Texans for Santa Anna."

———— ★ ————

After JFK and LBJ were elected in 1960, John F. Kennedy commented, "When we got into office, the thing that surprised me most was that things were just as bad as we'd been saying they were." Apparently, LBJ agreed.

Congressman Bill Sarpalius recalls an incident from his first campaign for state senator. He was going door to door and encountered an unenthusiastic voter. "When I knocked on this particular door, I heard some shuffling and noise from inside the house. I waited several minutes, then knocked again. I hated just to leave, so I waited and waited, and finally, the door opened very slowly.

"It was an old woman all bent over who opened the door but carefully kept the screen door latched. As she looked at me with squinted eyes in a little old wrinkled face, I said, 'Ma'am, my name is Bill Sarpalius and I'm running for the Texas Senate. I would like to give you a piece of my literature and ask for your vote in the upcoming election.'

"The woman looked up at me and declared, 'Young man, when you are 86 years old, you don't give a damn who your state senator is!' With that, she shut the door."

Political commentator Sam Attlesey recalls a former Dallas County commissioner who tried to explain why he lost a re-election bid. The reasons he gave were illness and fatigue. In other words, he said, the voters were "sick and tired" of him.

On rare occasions, campaigners actually embrace opponents' charges. Attlesey also relates a comment attributed to Edwin Edwards during the 1991 gubernatorial race in Louisiana, when Edwards ran against former Ku Klux Klan leader David Duke. While Duke was being blasted for his racist past and white-sheeted KKK activities, Edwards was the target of womanizing charges, charges that Edwards seemed almost proud of. Supposedly, this situation prompted Edwards to say, "The charges against Duke are unfair. Clearly I'm the real wizard in the sheets."

A candidate for county attorney out in West Texas received a slightly more subtle response when he asked a fellow for his vote. The man replied, "Well, to tell the truth, I never did think we really needed a county attorney. But I believe I could vote for you without compromising that viewpoint."

———— ★ ————

Deciding when and if to run for office is always a puzzle, and while Ann Richards was State Treasurer, she received a press inquiry about the prospects of her being a candidate for governor in the next election, which was still three years away. She responded as follows. "I'm reminded of a story told by Claude Pepper, the 87-year-old congressman from Florida. He said a stockbroker came up to him and said, 'This stock I'm offering to you is certain to quadruple in three years.' Claude looked at him and replied, 'Son, at my age I don't even buy green bananas.'"

———— ★ ————

Confronted with a hostile voter, the candidate's temptation is to make a snappy, in-kind reply. About the only time campaign etiquette permits that pleasure is with an out-and-out heckler. A classic is the time a heckler at a political rally shouted at a speaker, "Mister, I wouldn't vote for you if you were Saint Peter." Whereupon the candidate shouted back, "Feller, if I was Saint Peter, you wouldn't be in my district."

———— ★ ————

The late Will Burnett, longtime county judge of Hays County, told of another prize reaction. The candidate and his aide were campaigning through the countryside when they spotted a fellow working in a field near the road. Pulling over, the candidate got out and introduced himself to the fellow and started his pitch. After listening a few minutes, the farmer snarled, "Listen, I think you are a low-down, no-good reprobate, you're wasting my time, and I wouldn't vote for you if you were the last man on earth. Now go on, get out of here." Climbing back in his car, the candidate told his assistant, "Put that man down as doubtful."

———— ★ ————

Even a well-intended voter message may have mixed results. LBJ told about an Adlai Stevenson encounter with a staunch supporter who came up to him and exclaimed, "Governor, you are going to win because every thinking person in America is going to vote for you." Replied Adlai, "Oh, but that won't be enough. You know to win you have to have a majority."

———— ★ ————

Very occasionally, a politico gets a clean, safe shot at a deserving target. Sarah Weddington, who won the 1973 Roe v. Wade freedom-of-choice abortion case before the U. S. Supreme Court, enjoys telling about an incident at a hotel where a women's political meeting and a Texas Medical Association convention were going on at the same time. Weddington was in the elevator, and several doctors were behind her. "The doors opened and a woman got on, and she was wearing a badge," Sarah recalls. "One of the doctors said to her, 'You must be one of the libbers. What are you running for, sweetie?' And she said, 'I am the Governor's most recent appointee to the Texas Board of Medical Examiners. And what did you say your name was?'"

———— ★ ————

Candidates make mistakes, and some errors are unavoidable simply because of the warp speed of modern campaigning. But frankly, some errors occur because the candidate is dumb or the staff is incompetent. Whatever the cause, when errors occur, the media and opponents typically are not known for exhibiting magnanimous self-restraint. Normal responses are sadistic glee and celebration, and prolonged public humiliation of the blunderer.

———— ★ ————

In the 1990 gubernatorial campaign, education was a key issue in both parties' primary battles. On the Republican side, former Secretary of State Jack Rains had the misfortune of announcing with great fanfare a formal position paper on education. The prideful declaration of his Ten-Point Plan to Improve Texas Education turned to red-faced embarrassment, however, when the press noticed that the plan had only nine points.

———— ★ ————

Occasionally candidates say exactly the wrong thing at exactly the wrong time. As an old West Texas saying goes, "There's no use throwing chicken feathers at chickens." Houston lawyer and longtime State Democratic Executive Committee member Ed Cogburn tells two stories of candidates who made the wrong appeal to precisely the wrong audiences. The first was a state rep candidate who actually favored a teachers' pay raise, but in speaking to a statewide teacher's group, phrased his support this way: "The only reason we need a teacher pay raise is to get better teachers."

The second incident involved a lawyer who had the misfortune of running for state representative against a truck driver, and the greater misfortune of forgetting where he was when he addressed a Teamsters' meeting. He climaxed his pitch with what turned out to be an unintentionally devastating rhetorical question: "Who do you want to represent you: a lawyer who understands the law and can write good legislation, or a dumb trucker?"

———— ★ ————

Such a misstep can lead to what Molly Ivins quotes as an old East Texas saying to describe a delicate predicament: "Hair in the butter." It also can lead to continuous chanting of the politician's prayer: "Teach us to utter words that are tender and gentle, for tomorrow we may have to eat them."

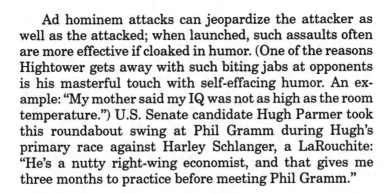

Ad hominem attacks can jeopardize the attacker as well as the attacked; when launched, such assaults often are more effective if cloaked in humor. (One of the reasons Hightower gets away with such biting jabs at opponents is his masterful touch with self-effacing humor. An example: "My mother said my IQ was not as high as the room temperature.") U.S. Senate candidate Hugh Parmer took this roundabout swing at Phil Gramm during Hugh's primary race against Harley Schlanger, a LaRouchite: "He's a nutty right-wing economist, and that gives me three months to practice before meeting Phil Gramm."

Former Attorney General Jim Mattox was as rugged as they come, but also provided a Texas-sized target for his opponents. Fringe candidate Republican gubernatorial hopeful Reverend W. N. Otwell shot far into outer space with this lunacy directed at Mattox: "I'm not necessarily saying the man's gay, I'm just saying he's wimpish. I think he's like a man who could possibly wear lace on his underwear." Subsequent speculation around the Capitol was that Mattox, whose apt campaign slogan was "Texas Tough," probably wore underwear made of burlap and cactus. Mattox opponent Roy Barrera, Jr. was more direct, claiming that Mattox brought "disgrace, fiscal irresponsibility and scandal to the office," though he hastened to add (i.e., clumsily dissemble) that he was not going to engage in mudslinging: "It's very appropriate for candidates to bring out the facts." Ann Richards had this reply to opponent Mattox's attacks about her non-answer on the drug-use question: "I feel very fortunate, truthfully, that there was a treatment program for my disease (alcoholism). I wish there were a treatment program for meanness, and then maybe Mattox could get well."

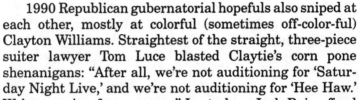

1990 Republican gubernatorial hopefuls also sniped at each other, mostly at colorful (sometimes off-color-ful) Clayton Williams. Straightest of the straight, three-piece suiter lawyer Tom Luce blasted Claytie's corn pone shenanigans: "After all, we're not auditioning for 'Saturday Night Live,' and we're not auditioning for 'Hee Haw.' We're running for governor." Last-place Jack Rains fired at Claytie, with no apparent effect: "This is not the time for Roy Rogers and the Sons of the Pioneers to be taking over Austin." Among the Republicans at least, 'Hee Haw' and Roy Rogers won.

Holier-than-thou posturing sometimes sells, sometimes doesn't. A better approach is that used by Land Commissioner Garry Mauro, who once cleverly poked fun at himself while at the same time staking out the high ethical ground on income-tax disclosure: "The people have a right to know how elected officials make — or, in my case, lose — their money."

Adlai Stevenson, undoubtedly one of the most principled men ever to run for president, phrased the principles-versustactics struggle this way: "The hardest thing about any political campaign is how to win without proving that you are unworthy of winning."

───── ★ ─────

Jake Pickle came by his fiscal conservatism honestly. One time while he was visiting his quite elderly father in Big Spring, he decided that his dad badly needed a replacement for the battered old Stetson he always wore. Knowing that his tightfisted father would never agree to pay what a really good hat cost these days, he conspired with the dry goods salesman in advance. "When I bring my dad in for a new hat, show him the best Stetson you have, and when he asks the cost, tell him it's $25. Then later I'll pay you the difference." This scenario was played as planned except that Jake's father, when told the price, said, "Say, that does seem like a pretty good deal. Tell you what, I'll take two."

Consultants come in all different shapes, forms, and morality levels. Houston trial lawyer Wayne Fisher tells this story to explain what a political consultant is. A fellow had a Persian cat who was causing problems in the neighborhood, producing lots of kittens. A neighbor complained about the cat roaming around at night and engaging in that kind of conduct. The result was that the owner had the cat neutered. A few weeks later the neighbor ran into the cat owner and said, "Well, I guess you took care of the cat and he's not out roaming around at night anymore." The owner replied, "No, he's still at it and he's still roaming around, but now he's just a consultant."

Phillip Adams had this dart for modern image makers: "Advertising men and politicians are dangerous if they are separated. Together they are diabolical."

Generally, in 1988 in the South, wherever Lloyd Bentsen could help the Democratic ticket, Dukakis could hurt; wherever Bentsen was a sail, Dukakis was a bottom-dragging anchor. Atlanta pollster Claibourne Darden commented on Bentsen's lack of impact in the South: "That is not necessarily Lloyd Bentsen's fault. You can't make a possum look like a bird dog." Whether Bentsen or Dukakis was supposed to be the possum, many Texas Democrats came to view Dukakis's campaign operation as some sort of road-kill. Indeed, the Dukakis presidential campaign in 1988 was one of the most famous consultancy debacles in recent Texas political history. Despite having on the ticket Texan Lloyd Bentsen, legendary for his own effective management and leadership of a statewide coordinated campaign in 1982, the Dukakis inner circle — sometimes referred to in Texas as the inert circle — cleverly decide to import a bunch of whiz-kid Yankee know-it-all's to teach Texans how to campaign in Texas. Abstractly considered, that was a profoundly bad idea. In practice, it was worse.

A Bentsen aide tells this story to illustrate the results. One of the young Yankee whizzers traveled off to East Texas to educate the ineducable. Along the way, he stopped at a roadside cafe and decided to try out one of the foods that his new Texas acquaintances had recommended so highly, but that he had never before sampled. Dressed in new-bought boots and borrowed faded jeans, he was doing his best to fit in, even to the point of trying to mimic the waitress's deep twang. Boston and Tyler being a fur' piece apart, his verbal gymnastics weren't very convincing, but the waitress managed to keep a straight face until at last he finished reading the menu and ordered one of the famous chicken fried steaks. She lost it, though, when he ended his order with this request: "And ma'am, please tell the chef to prepare that steak medium rare."

———— ★ ————

Fortunately, in at least some rural Texas House races, consultants are still the exception. There a more pleasant naivete prevails. Rep. Steve Wolens tells of the time he was driving a newly elected colleague from the Capitol to the Austin airport so they could catch a flight to Dallas. "I was going on and on about my friend, George Shipley, and how wonderful he was. Finally, my new friend asked me who was this guy George Shipley. 'He's a well-known pollster,' I replied. 'Oh yeah,' said the new representative quite seriously, 'What does he upholster?'"

On the subject of travel, the immensity of Texas takes its toll on any statewide campaign. It's 767 miles from Brownsville to Amarillo, 825 miles from El Paso to Port Arthur. Literally, the Texas campaign trail is a mighty long trail, and these days air travel is an absolute necessity.

Native Texan Bruce Babbitt, who became Governor of Arizona, figures in a Mo Udall travel story. Despite the fact that Udall had only one good eye, Mo owned and operated a single-engine airplane. On this particular occasion, he had asked Babbitt if he wanted to ride with him in his plane to Tucson.

"I was wearing an eyepatch at the time," Udall explains. "Bruce looked at my patch and then at the plane and said, 'No, I don't fly in single-engine airplanes with one-eyed pilots because of my back.' I told him I didn't know he had a back problem. 'It's not that exactly,' he said. 'It's just that I have a yellow stripe down the middle of it.'"

Texas is diverse, as well as large, and has what Molly Ivins calls a "mosaic of cultures." Over three million Texans live in poverty, but Texas has more than its fair share of oil zillionaires and $400-an-hour lawyers. Texas has the fifth highest illiteracy rate in the country, but Austin regularly is ranked as the city with the highest average educational level in the nation. The contrasts abound and stagger. Molly concludes, more simply, "The cultures are black, Chicano, Southern, freak, suburban, and shitkicker. (Shitkicker is dominant.) They are all rotten for women. Humanism is not alive and well in Texas."

Coming to grips with the unprecedented boom-and-bust decade of the 1980's challenged the state's most creative political consultants. Lemming-like waves of fortune-hunting Yankees swept over the state during the boom, then receded as oil and real estate markets collapsed. For a time, over 50 percent of the voters in Austin had lived in the city for less than ten years; 25 percent, less than five years. Urban residency and voting patterns spun around like tops. Consultants and candidates tried to come to grips with yuppies and new-collar voters. Democratic political consultant Ralph Whitehead described the difference between a new-collar voter and a Yuppie thusly: "You can tell a new-collar voter about $600 toilet seats at the defense department and he'll want to fire people involved. You tell a Yuppie about one and he'll want to know what colors they come in."

Some folks say that the relationship between politicians and issues tends to be inverse: as issues get tougher, politicians get weaker; the more challenging the issues become, the lower the politicians duck. The reason is survival. Find the officeholder who constantly seeks out the most controversial issues of the day on which to opine, and your political actuarial table will reveal a very short political life-expectancy indeed.

The great mayor of San Antonio and New Deal congressman Maury Maverick, Sr. defined democracy as "liberty plus groceries." He pointed out that the delicate trick of balancing idealism and pocketbook is a feat beyond the ability of most performers in the political circus. Maverick himself would send his fellow liberals an inscription in Maverick Latin: "Illigitimi non carborundum." Translation: "Don't let the bastards grind you down."

———— ★ ————

Maverick's wholesale commitment to New Deal liberalism exceeded that of his political base. Lyndon Johnson said Maverick just "got out ahead of his voters." Maverick knew that, too, but maintained a good humor on the subject. In a time when racism was dominant among many Texas voters, Maverick could tease: "I am so liberal that I say 'chigro' instead of chigger."

———— ★ ————

His son, Maury Maverick, Jr. followed in his footsteps as a liberal Texas legislator and as a tireless defender of civil liberties, in the legislature and in the courtroom. Once when Maury, Jr. was in the House, he was asked to introduce U.S. Senator Joe McCarthy, who was to give a speech to the legislature. Maverick replied that he would be glad to make the introduction, but only if he could substitute Mickey Mouse for McCarthy. "If we are going to get a rat to talk to us, at least let's get a good rat." His proposal received 55 votes.

Deeply committed, the Mavericks could be hard on themselves and on others. The story is told of a hospital visit by Maury, Jr. to his father, who had just suffered a severe heart attack. He entered the hospital room and his dad motioned him to the bedside.

Senior: You know, son, this is it.

Junior: Yes, papa, I know.

Senior: Son, you and I have never been very close.

Junior: I know, papa. I know.

Senior: I think it may have been my fault, but I want you to know that I am proud of you, son.

Junior: Well, thank you, papa.

Senior: Yes, son, I am real proud of you — I am proud that you didn't turn out to be a complete horse's ass like Elliott Roosevelt.

Generally fearless in the face of controversy, Maverick the younger also had no qualms about telling his friends when they went wrong, but usually served up that message with a winning twist of humor. Civil rights lawyer and Houston Democratic leader Arthur Gochman tells the story of the time Maury, Jr. wrote a letter to Fidel Castro in Cuba after Castro had overthrown the dictator Batista and assumed power. Castro made a statement that if one American soldier stepped foot on Cuban soil he would "kill 100 gringos." Maverick wrote a lengthy, passionate treatise, analyzing Cuban history and Cuba's position in the modern world, and attempting to persuade Castro that he really had no need for that sort of thing. Then, after making his impassioned but logical plea, he ended the letter with this turn: "But if you decide to go through with this, here is my suggestion for the top 100."

A similar story is told about the politician who was rushed to the hospital after being bitten by a rabid dog. The doctor entered the emergency room to conduct an examination and found the man furiously scribbling on a legal pad. The wound was superficial and easily cleansed, and the doctor said there was little chance of serious infection or death "so you can stop writing your will." The man replied: "Oh, I'm not writing a will at all. I'm just making a list of the people I want to bite."

The Mavericks exemplified the virtues of strongly held positions and strongly expressed commitments, as their political defeats showed the harshness of electoral realities. Richard Henderson, Maury Maverick, Sr.'s biographer, also attributed Maury Sr.'s defeat to taking "too many liberties with a normally conservative constituency."

Weathervane neutrality is the opposite of kamikaze ideological fervor, but can be equally hazardous. Dante predicted that "the hottest places in hell are reserved for those who, in a time of great moral crisis, maintain their neutrality." The all-time classic Texas statement on this point is Jim Hightower's: "There ain't nothing in the middle of the road but yellow stripes and dead armadillos."

Hightower also took a good shot at rhetorical dissemblers, those who adopt catch-phrases without the underlying philosophy. "Saying 'populist' 15 times in your speech doesn't make you a populist. You can put ribbons on a skunk, but it's still going to stink up the place."

Overall, Texans like strength in their politicians, straight talk, clear and simple and honest — or at least the illusion thereof. West Texas is full of such sayings: "You can't raise cattle by shooting the bull." "It takes more than hot air to turn a windmill." "When a rattlesnake strikes, kick the snake or kick the bucket."

Candidates don't often get to pick the issues. Sometimes the voter's job is to separate the officeholders from the issues. As publishing magnate and pundit extraordinaire Sam Kinch, Jr. quoted from an anti-branch banking election brochure: "Letting the fox in the hen house to guard the chickens generally results in larger foxes and fewer eggs."

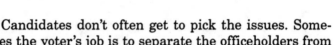

An issue that still raises dust in many parts of Texas is the age-old temperance debate, wet vs. dry. A former state senator from Dallas tells this line from a wet/dry election held in Oak Cliff in Dallas County back in the early '60s. At a public forum on the issue, one woman was urging everyone to vote against having Oak Cliff go from dry to wet. Finally, she declared with feeling, "I'd rather commit adultery than allow alcohol to be served in Oak Cliff."

Whereupon some wag sitting in the audience, in a clearly audible stage whisper added, "Who the hell wouldn't?"

In many parts of the state, Texas politics wouldn't be the same without Texas Baptists. San Antonio columnist Roddy Stinson made a comment during the presidential campaign of (Baptist) Democrat Jimmy Carter that pretty much holds true to this day in many parts of Texas: "Being a Baptist in Georgia is like being a virgin. Even if you aren't one, you say you are because you can't be elected homecoming queen or governor or anything else otherwise."

─────── ★ ───────

Assistant Texas Attorney General Dave Bolduc shares this Earl Long story about the practicalities of religion and politics. When Earl was Governor of Louisiana he gave a speech in a parish where half the voters were Catholic, half Baptist. Cagey pol that he was, he began by saying that the most pleasant times of his youth were on Sunday mornings when he would hitch a pair of horses to the family wagon and drive his grandmother and grandfather to the Catholic Church. When the service was over, "Uncle Earl" continued, he would return home, hook up a fresh team and drive his other grandmother and grandfather to the Baptist Church.

After the speech when he and his aide were driving back home, Long's aide said, "Governor, I didn't know you had a Catholic grandfather and grandmother." Uncle Earl replied, "Hell, we didn't even have a wagon."

─────── ★ ───────

Modern campaigns are awesomely expensive. Jesse Unruh said, "Money is the mother's milk of politics," and Mark Hanna made the same point: "There are two things that are important in politics. The first is money, and I can't remember what the second is." The 1990 gubernatorial campaigns collectively spent $32.5 million. Campaigns weren't always so costly. Oran Milo Roberts, Texas Governor from 1879 to 1883, spent 35 cents on his political campaign to be elected governor. Governor Ma Ferguson was elected Governor of Texas in 1924, in part on a platform promising the bargain of "two governors for the price of one," in reliance on her husband, former Governor Jim Ferguson, who was barred from state office after having been impeached and removed in 1917. (Ma defeated a Ku Klux Klan candidate, Felix Robertson, and was defeated for reelection in 1926 and in 1930, but made a comeback in 1932.)

——— ★ ———

Earl Long told this story to illustrate fund-raising problems. One Sunday a country preacher gave a thunderous fire-and-brimstone sermon. The audience listened with rapt attention, and afterwards, feeling confident that he had inspired his flock, the preacher directed the passing of the collections plate. It passed slowly along the pews and finally came back to the preacher. He looked down and, to his surprise and disappointment, he saw that the plate was empty. Immediately he looked straight up to the heavens and shouted at the top of his lungs, "Praise the Lord that this plate got out of this crowd safely!"

——— ★ ———

People-oriented, anti-special interests candidates often learn to campaign on a shoestring budget. Legendary Texas state senator and congressman Henry B. Gonzalez tells this story. "I've always campaigned with little or no money and in every serious contest I've faced overwhelming financial strength on the other side. Most of my strong supporters have been about as broke as me, but they're always enthusiastic workers. In one of my campaigns, the opposition had the luxury I couldn't dream of: paid precinct workers.

"One of my best friends got the call: the magnificent sum of $25 per day for precinct work. He needed the money, but he was my supporter. What to do?

"My friend called me with his problem. 'Can I take the money but work for you, Henry?' I said, 'Sure, and tell everybody else the same thing.' He did, and I won in a landslide." Henry B. always wins in a landslide.

——— ★ ———

Another story of Henry B.'s enthusiastic campaign workers involved his first race for state representative in 1950. On election day an old family friend spotted Henry outside the polling place and came running up to him, shouting excitedly: "Henry, Henry, I just voted for you but, for your father's sake, now you must help me get my citizenship papers."

A key strategy for master fund-raisers is to develop a corps of loyal contributors who can be counted on to contribute time after time, campaign after campaign. Former Democratic National Committee Chairman Bob Strauss is one of the best at this, as illustrated by this story he told at a 1987 Democratic Leadership Council meeting. Strauss was complimenting the generosity of loyal contributor Ben Alexander. "A few years ago I wrote Ben and asked him for some money for a candidate and a cause. And he wrote back and said: 'Bob, I dislike that candidate intensely and I am against the cause. However, I have checked my records and over the past 20-odd years, I have given you close to $50,000 in response to 31 requests, without ever having turned you down. Therefore, despite the fact that I despise what you are standing for, to keep my record intact, here is $250.'"

Incidentally, multidimensional talent that Strauss was, his wife had an excellent retort guaranteed to prevent him from developing an overinflated ego. One day he was wondering aloud how many "truly wise men" there were in the world. Her reply was, "That's hard to tell, but I imagine there's one less than you think there is."

Ann Richards tells a Mae West story to illustrate the "virtues" of Democratic grass roots fund-raising. Mae West ran into one of her old chums who was wearing a brand-new, full-length mink coat. "Where did you get that, honey?" asked Mae. "I met a man with $10,000," replied the other woman. A year later, Mae met the woman again. This time it was Mae West who had on a brand new full length mink coat. "Did you find a man with $10,000?" asked the friend. "No, honey, I met 10,000 men with a dollar," replied Mae.

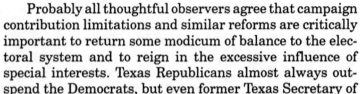

Probably all thoughtful observers agree that campaign contribution limitations and similar reforms are critically important to return some modicum of balance to the electoral system and to reign in the excessive influence of special interests. Texas Republicans almost always outspend the Democrats, but even former Texas Secretary of State and Republican gubernatorial candidate Jack Rains argued: "$25,000 is about all the good government an individual should be able to afford in any 12-month period."

———— ★ ————

Not surprisingly, Dallas billionaire H. Ross Perot has been a large contributor to several political races. Federal judge and legal humorist Jerry Buchmeyer recited this (probably) apocryphal news item concerning Perot's most recent philanthropy. "Dallas billionaire H. Ross Perot shocked the entire human race today with the announcement that he had purchased the Lord God Almighty, believed by many to be the creator of the universe. No purchase price was disclosed, either by Perot or by the ancient but still serviceable deity, who is best remembered for creating the heavens and the earth in only six days —

a feat Perot describes as 'pretty darn impressive, especially for someone with no money.'

"Perot also announced there would be no immediate changes in the requirements for salvation. 'You've still got to pass through the eye of the needle if you want to play your harp in Heaven,' Perot said. 'No pass, no play.'"

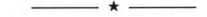

Political fund-raisers have their own etiquette. Special manners and customs have evolved through the centuries to create and maintain an appearance of placid civility that only occasionally succeeds in concealing what is in reality a seething caldron of frenetic egos, frustrated agendas, and mutual exploitation — all for a good cause, of course! *Austin American Statesman* editor and political anthropologist Arnold Garcia has cataloged many of the basic rules of deportment as follows.

> Arrival and departure. There are two reasons people show up at fund-raisers: to see and be seen. Arriving 30 minutes after the event is scheduled to start is considered chic. Make sure the candidate sees you, then go about your real business. If you must impress people with how busy you are, look at your watch every 10 minutes or so and start for the door 30 minutes after you get there, but make sure people see you leaving.
>
> No sense in wasting that performance with a discreet exit.
>
> If you want to miss the candidate's speech, arrive 45 minutes after the event is supposed to start.
>
> Dress. The most important thing you can wear to a fund-raiser is deodorant. Particularly in warm weather. That's because candidates are

notorious for booking events in small rooms. Political wisdom is that a big crowd packed in a tiny room is better than the opposite.

The second-most important item of attire is the name tag provided at the door. There is some difference of opinion on whether you should wear a name tag on the right or left shoulder, but not wearing one is considered bad form.

Austin is still pretty laid back, so dress comfortably. Fund-raiser Susan Krute cautions, however, that cutoffs and sandals are inappropriate for events held "above the third floor."

Greeting people. It is considered bad form to stare at somebody's name tag because it tells them instantly that you don't know who they are, and political players tend to be egotistical. A name tag is a billboard, not an encyclopedia, so glance at it and keep driving.

You will probably run across somebody you've met before but don't remember where or when. In that instance, the appropriate greeting is "Nice to see you." Even more appropriate — especially if you're sure you've met before but can't read the name tag — is "Nice to see you again."

Fatal greeting, particularly for officeholders, is "How nice to meet you."

Greeting the candidate. Don't hog his or her time. A candidate is being tugged in as many directions as there are people at those things, so don't spend time talking about your philosophy on potholes or the current presidential administration. The candidate's not listening anyway.

However, if you walk into the fund-raiser and see no one there, don't make the candidate feel even worse by saying something like: "Did everyone leave already?" Even worse: "Am I early?" Travis County Commissioner Pam Reed suggests saying something like "What a lovely room." Though tempting, resist the urge to survey the empty room and say, "My, don't you look natural."

Shaking hands and hugging and kissing. A vigorous handshake will get you in trouble. That's because you're liable to spill somebody's beer. A modest peck on the cheek is considered appropriate in greeting members of the opposite gender. If you know them well enough to say, "Nice to see you again," that is.

Conversation. Keep it light, and keep it brief. You really mark yourself as an amateur if you try to engage someone in serious conversation. People talk for an average of 90 seconds at fund-raisers, but don't get caught looking around to see who else is there while you're doing it. Focusing on somebody's right eye is good way to look past them without being obvious.

Name dropping. It's standard practice, but watch yourself. In that same vein, it's gauche — but it's done — to holler "Hey, Ann" or "Hey, Bob" across the room even if you've never met the governor or lieutenant governor. It might impress someone who hears you do it and it's risk-free.

That's because Ann or Bob will return your greeting with "Nice to see you."

——————— ★ ———————

An issue of considerable recent debate in Texas is the proposal for term limitations for certain elected offices. One observer has called this a "default issue," arguing that the only persons who really seem to be enthusiastic about term limitations are persons who've never had a term — perhaps they can win by default. On the other side of the issue is this statement by one of the proponents of such limits: "Politicians are like manure. If you keep them in a big pile, they'll stay there and stink. You have to spread them around."

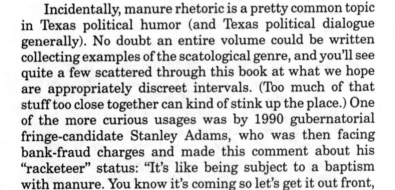

Incidentally, manure rhetoric is a pretty common topic in Texas political humor (and Texas political dialogue generally). No doubt an entire volume could be written collecting examples of the scatological genre, and you'll see quite a few scattered through this book at what we hope are appropriately discreet intervals. (Too much of that stuff too close together can kind of stink up the place.) One of the more curious usages was by 1990 gubernatorial fringe-candidate Stanley Adams, who was then facing bank-fraud charges and made this comment about his "racketeer" status: "It's like being subject to a baptism with manure. You know it's coming so let's get it out front, get it over with and get on to more important things." Now, exactly how did he ever come up with that comparison? And why?

On the campaign trail, politicians and press have a love-hate relationship. They need each other. Politicians need name i.d., which the press can give. Politicians also want a good reputation, which the press can give or take away — though as Texas Supreme Court Justice Bob Gammage was fond of saying when he was in Congress, "I don't care what they say about me, as long as they spell my name right." On the other hand, the press needs politicians in order to have something, preferably something negative, to write about. Austin TV anchorman and marketing mogul Neal Spelce likes to quote Jody Powell's description of political columnists: "A political columnist is someone who watches a conflict from a safe distance and then comes down from the hills to shoot the wounded."

Another observer defined the interview process this way: a contest in which the journalist attempts to take advantage of the politician's pleasure in hearing himself talk, and the politician attempts to take advantage of the journalist's gullibility.

The press arsenal bristles with diverse weaponry. The press can destroy an officeholder with one nuclear war-headed story or can administer an excruciating Chinese water torture. Lawyer Joe Nagy observed when he was leaving office after serving as president of the State Bar: "The press is like a bunch of chiggers — they won't eat you but they'll bite you where it's embarrassing to scratch." Another State Bar president characterized his own favorite press outlet: "Back home, we have a bird called the cowbird. It spends all of its waking hours following cattle, pecking through manure, or sitting astride the cow seeking ticks. It is so concerned in its search for minutiae to swallow, it never sees the effort and progress the cow makes to survive, produce, or move. The cow could live without the bird; the bird would starve without the cow. I've often wondered if [the publication] has the capacity to rise above pecking through manure or searching for ticks."

Almost every officeholder has spewed invective, at least in private, against the press. A typical LBJ gibe was: "The fact that a man is a newspaper reporter is evidence of some flaw of character."

On the other hand, Maury Maverick, Sr. pointed out the decidedly mixed-bag of power and poverty that political journalists carry: "Newspapermen are the most underpaid and overprivileged guys in the world." Maverick, incidentally, was a great believer in the power of the written word, and once introduced legislation to create for military enlistees a required reading list concerning the horrors of war.

Former journalist and Texas Commissioner of Agriculture Jim Hightower took this self-effacing, but well-aimed, shot during an address to the National Press Club: "When I entered politics I took the only downward turn you could take from journalism."

A true story about Hightower during the 1990 elections demonstrates both the power of the media and the Hightower name i.d.: "The power of television: 36% of Texans surveyed by pollster Bryan Eppstein in October said that they had seen Agriculture Commissioner Jim Hightower's TV ads. 17% of the respondents liked the ad, 8% didn't, 5% had mixed impressions and 6% were undecided. The problem was, Hightower didn't run any TV commercials."

Another true story about a poll involved a "voter i.d." telephone project, in which callers attempted to determine gubernatorial preferences of likely voters. A pollster reached an elderly lady in Nacogdoches and asked her how she would vote in the governor's race. She replied, "Oh, I never vote. It just encourages them."

Almost everyone who has been a participant in or otherwise closely associated with events that have attracted media attention has at some point been appalled by the errors and inaccuracies in press reports. One current legislator defines journalism as "a profession that takes it upon itself to explain to others what it doesn't understand, doesn't want to understand, and isn't capable of understanding."

The press sometimes seems to cherish vulgarity above all else. Once Bob Bullock observed what seemed to be a little too much press glee over his predicament in being hospitalized for removal of hemorrhoids. His facetious press release included this clarification of his hospitalization: "The keen scatological interest of most reporters originally prompted me to schedule the operation in the Capitol press room. My doctors, however, advised me to seek more sanitary conditions."

Senator Carl Parker delivered a similar ribbing once when the Austin Police Department received a telephoned bomb threat indicating that a bomb was hidden somewhere in the Capitol and was scheduled to annihilate the Legislature sometime before noon. Responding to a warning to leave the premises, Parker paused at the Press

Room long enough to give this advice: "The public has a right to know the exact time the bomb goes off. I think ya'll should stay till then to provide complete and accurate coverage." The alarm was false.

——————— ★ ———————

The high esteem with which the press regard public officeholders is reflected in this time-honored advice from H. L. Mencken: "There is only one way for a newspaperman to look at a politician, and that is down." President Johnson reciprocated the feeling when Vietnam dove Senator Frank Church appeared at a White House reception.

"Where do you get your ideas on Vietnam?" asked LBJ.

"From Walter Lippmann," Church answered.

Johnson huffed, "Next time you need a dam in Idaho, you just go ask Walter Lippmann."

——————— ★ ———————

Johnson's press secretary, Bill Moyers, gave this dual description of honesty: "There are honest journalists like there are honest politicians. When bought they stay bought."

——————— ★ ———————

Political journalists have developed their own specialized language — so specialized, in fact, that the most talented of the species can say two things at once, simultaneously communicating one message to the public at large and another message to political insiders. To accomplish this, journalists use code. *Austin American Statesman* editor, and political commentator extraordinaire, Arnold Garcia, has disclosed parts of that code, and he provides the following translations of pol-journspeak:

Grass-roots (as in "grass-roots candidate") — a broke candidate.

Grass-roots organization — a group of people who aspire one day to be grass-roots candidates.

Populist — a grass-roots candidate who accidentally got elected.

Activist (as in "community activist") — unemployed gadfly.

Consultant — activist with a temporary job.

Firebrand (as in "firebrand activist") — loudmouth.

Underdog (as in "underdog candidate") — this joker would figure out a way to lose even if his or her name was the only one on the ballot.

Perennial (as in "perennial candidate") — this joker has demonstrated nothing beyond the inability to take a hint.

Well-connected (as in "the well-connected candidate") — this individual may be a jerk, but he or she is a rich jerk.

Low-profile (as in "low-profile race") — who cares?

High-profile (as in "high-profile race") — the reporter cares.

Fiscal conservative — 1. (obsolete usage:) this joker should be wearing a brown shirt and an armband. 2. (current usage:) this joker went broke in business and now wants to run a government, for a salary.

Source — the person who hands out press releases.

Reliable source — the person who types press releases.

Informed source — the person who ordered the reliable source to type the press release.

Political observers — 1. (if the reporter is on an out-of-town assignment:) — the cabbie who drives the reporter from the airport to the hotel is one. 2. (normal usage:) the reporter's bartender and drinking buddies.

Knowledgeable observers — what political observers become after three drinks.

Controversial (as in "the controversial proposal") — knowledgeable observers don't like it.

Insiders (as in "political insiders speculate") — four people — usually with titles — who talk regularly with the reporter.

Earthy (as in "the earthy candidate") — a candidate who sprinkles the "f" word liberally into private conversation.

Colorful (as in "the colorful candidate") — 1. different. 2. exotic. 3. nuts. Veteran (as in "the veteran officeholder") — should have retired 10 years ago.

Aggressive (as in "the candidate is running an aggressive campaign") — mean.

————— ★ —————

For the lucky candidate, at the end of the campaign trail is electoral bliss: election. Former Texas Lieutenant Governor Bill Hobby described the effect of a formal election certificate: "It's a marvelous piece of paper. It improves your personality. Your jokes are funnier when you have one of those things." The resulting flattery and courting can be hazardous to the new officeholder's health, however, and Ambrose Bierce aptly warned, "Flattery is like perfume, it is nice to smell, but it should not be swallowed."

————— ★ —————

Officeholding can be pleasure or pain. When Lincoln presented the Emancipation Proclamation to the members of his cabinet, they unanimously opposed it. He simply exercised his presidential prerogative: "On this issue the nays have seven, the ayes have one — the ayes have it."

On the minus side of the balance was the famous observation of Vice President John Nance ("Cactus Jack") Garner, who appraised the vice presidency this way: "It's not worth a bucket of warm spit." Some historians insist the substance Garner alluded to was other than spit. In a kinder mood Garner described his office as "the spare tire on the automobile of government." On still another occasion Cactus Jack told this story: "Two brothers were born to a family in Kentucky. When they grew up, one ran off to sea, the other became Vice President of the United States. Neither one was ever heard from again."

After the 1990 election, Comptroller Bob Bullock said that his new job as Lt. Gov.-Elect was "kind of like being an unemployed king."

Finally, here's a true story Ann Richards tells about an early encounter after she had taken office for the first time as County Commissioner.

> When I first ran for Travis County Commissioner, I ran against the incumbent. It was a hard-fought race and when I won, the men on the road and bridge crew were fearful I was going to fire the lot of them since they had heard I was a regular Dragon Lady. Of course, I had no intention of firing a good crew, and I decided that as soon as I took office, I'd go out to what is called

the Precinct Barn and allay their fears. When I arrived, I was greeted, if that is the word, by a sullen and very quiet group of men — and one mangy, beaten-down old cur dog. We all went into the barn, but for the life of me, I couldn't get the men to say much. To break the ice, I asked them about their dog.

"What's its name?"

A few moments of silence passed when finally from the back of the room someone sheepishly called out, "You're gonna find out sooner or later, her name is Ann Richards."

Whereupon a young man in the front quickly interjected, "But we call her Miss Ann!"

We didn't have any problems after that.

CHAPTER THREE

Politics and Politicians

W e need politicians. As Harry Truman said, a politician is someone "who understands government, and it takes a politician to run the government." Nonetheless, the terms "politics" and "politicians" too often are used as pejoratives. In fact, one standard dictionary definition of politician is "a person who seeks to gain power or advancement within an organization in ways that are generally disapproved."

Fortunately, humor softens at least some of the criticism. A little bit. Less delicately than Truman, Brendan Francis made the same point about the indispensability of politicians: "Politicians, like prostitutes, are held in contempt. But what man does not run to them when he needs their services?" More typical was H. L. Mencken's remark: "A good politician is quite as unthinkable as an honest burglar."

What about statesmen? Perhaps they're better. Once again, Truman gave the definitive answer in his terse Midwestern style: "A statesman is a politician who's been dead ten or fifteen years. A similar, slightly more demanding definition is Thomas Reed's: "A statesman is a successful politician who is dead." Other definitions recognize that statesmanship is in the eye of the beholder. David Lloyd George defined a politician as "someone with whose politics you don't agree; if you agree with him he is a statesman." Other standard descriptions identify a politician as "someone who belongs to the opposite party" or someone "who stands for what he thinks others will fall for" or, as Oscar Wilde said, "An animal who can sit on a fence and yet keep both ears to the ground." Georges Pompidou differentiated the two species this way: "A statesman is a politician who places himself at the service of the nation. A politician is a statesman who places the nation at his service."

Even a statesman may be unappreciated. Maury Maverick, Sr. gave this advice to a young congressman: "Everything you do that is new or that inconveniences anybody will bring self-righteous criticism, pious warnings. Often when you act as a true statesman you will be ridiculed and thought a fool."

A politician who changes position on an issue, whether because of intelligent reevaluation of the position or because of evolving circumstances, risks being called a liar, or worse. An age-old question goes: How do you tell when a politician is lying? Watch his lips. When they start moving, that's it.

But in this era of daily polling and instant analysis, stolid perseverance in a position that becomes unpopular is rare. Even Cicero observed that "persistence in one opinion has never been considered a merit among political leaders."

The most recent Texas officeholder to fall prey to the accusation of indecisiveness was former Governor Mark White. Molly Ivins gave this analysis: "The man's peerless imitation of a weather vane has helped spread the impression that he can't go to the bathroom without consulting the polls. It's hard to look up to a fellow who always has his ear to the ground." Another White critic characterized him with this old definition of politician: "A politician is someone who shakes your hand before an election and your confidence afterwards." Representative Mike McKinney described White's leadership style thusly: "He's kind of like eating an artichoke without the sauce, just real bland."

★

When Bob Bullock was Comptroller, he made this proposal for candidate truth-testing: "All candidates for public office — new or used — ought to have to take truth serum before they get up to make a political speech and ought to have to take a lie detector test when they're through." (For the record, note that when Bullock made that statement, he was unopposed.)

Scoring pretty low on Bullock's own truth test standard was a wonderful letter sent out by his deputy Glen Castlebury to a somewhat irate citizen who had written Bullock to express doubt that Bullock personally read the letters his office received or personally composed the responses mailed out.

Dear Mr. Hicks:

You are right. Bob Bullock did not read your letters and Bob Bullock did not compose the replies.

You see, there is no Bob Bullock.

For the past 12 years, the image and media character of "Comptroller Bob Bullock" has been a grand P.R. hoax concocted and kept alive by the Creative Advertising Arts class at the University of Texas at Alpine. It was patterned after what LaSalle University did with the J. Edgar Hoover character.

That explains why you "see" Bob Bullock in press releases and film clips but never in person.

Actually, there once was a real Bob Bullock. He was Texas' Secretary of State back in 1972 but he died shortly after endorsing George McGovern for President and has been entombed since then in a quiet corner of the State Cemetery under the name of one of his ex-wives.

I reveal these things to you now because the University is dropping this project at the end of the spring semester because the Comptroller will not certify enough money to continue the P.R. project.

In the meantime, I am in control, and I am taking your situation under advisement.

Sincerely,

G. Martin Castlebury

Lies can take on a life of their own and almost instantly so on the campaign trail. One of the most successful Texas political emigrants is Willie Brown, the longtime Speaker of the California Assembly. According to ace political reporter Sam Attlesey, Brown has succinctly stated this truth about lies: "In politics, a lie unanswered becomes truth within 24 hours." Many Democrats felt that the 1988 Dukakis campaign foundered in large part because it failed to recognize and respond to this truism.

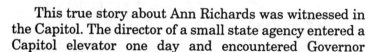

This true story about Ann Richards was witnessed in the Capitol. The director of a small state agency entered a Capitol elevator one day and encountered Governor Richards for the first time.

In her usual enthusiastic manner, the director gushed, "Governor, I'm so happy to see you! My mother keeps asking me if I've seen you. I told her I work at the Capitol a lot, and she keeps asking me if I've seen you and I keep telling her I haven't, and I know she thinks I'm a liar. Now I can tell her I've really seen Ann Richards and she won't think I'm a liar!"

As the elevator stopped and the door opened, Governor Richards placed her arm around the young woman's shoulders and leaned toward her confidentially, saying: "Don't you worry about it, honey. . . . The Capitol is full of liars."

--------- ★ ---------

Another somewhat cynical, or perhaps cynically realistic, observer has remarked that "Politicians who wish to succeed must be prepared to dissemble, at times to lie. In politics some deceit or moral dishonesty is the oil without which the machinery would not work."

--------- ★ ---------

Churchill offered another great truth about truth, or more specifically, about people ignoring the truth: "Men occasionally stumble over the truth, but most of them pick themselves up and hurry off as if nothing had happened." Wolcott Gibbs had this line about someone who was a little too fast and loose with the truth: "He wasn't exactly hostile to the facts, but he was apathetic about them."

--------- ★ ---------

Akin to misrepresenting or ignoring the truth is the well-established political tradition of stating partial truths. Senator Everett M. Dirksen of Illinois told the following story to illustrate the accusation against then Senate Majority Leader Lyndon Johnson. "The statement made by the majority leader on a number of occasions on the floor and in the tables he inserted in the [Congressional] Record are quite correct so far as they go. As I said before, however, it is like the man who fell off the twentieth floor of a building. As he passed the sixth floor a friend shouted to him, 'Mike, so far you're all right.' So, I believe in the interest of the whole rather than in the fraction of the story."

——————— ★ ———————

Even lobbyists — who by stereotype at least, are not usually lumped together as paragons of ethical sensitivity — have expressed disappointment at times with legislative truth-telling. This was a lobbyist comment overheard one day in the Texas Senate lounge: "Politicians are like a bunch of bananas. They are pretty yellow, they are all a little crooked, and they hang together."

——————— ★ ———————

The food analogies get worse. One of the best of the worst is about two cannibals who were discussing their favorite foods. One said he liked eating missionaries because the meat was so tender and sweet. The second cannibal agreed but declared that for really zestful eating, you can't beat politicians. "Hey, that's true all right," responded cannibal number one, "but ain't they hell to clean?"

——————— ★ ———————

Another recipe provides, "Render any politician down and there's quite enough fat to fry an egg."

——————— ★ ———————

Politicians have been compared to a veritable menagerie of what are, for the most part, pretty unseemly representatives of the animal kingdom. Ambrose Bierce declared that a politician is "an eel in the fundamental mud upon which the superstructure of organized society is reared." Even worse: "A politician is like a bullfrog — what ain't stomach is head, and that's mostly mouth." Still messier: "A politician is like a cockroach — it isn't what he eats and carries off, it's what he falls into and messes up."

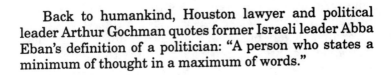

Back to humankind, Houston lawyer and political leader Arthur Gochman quotes former Israeli leader Abba Eban's definition of a politician: "A person who states a minimum of thought in a maximum of words."

———— ★ ————

Many politicians are quick studies, though some are just lazy studies. Former U.S. Speaker of the House Jim Wright tells about the late veteran Congressman Bob Poage, one of the most conscientious, hardworking, and knowledgeable members. When a new member asked Jim's opinion on a particular agricultural issue, Jim suggested that the member talk to Bob Poage. "He knows more about it than any of the rest of us." The freshman member, however, had already been exposed to one exhaustive and exhausting Poage lecture. He shook his head and said, "Thanks, but I really don't want to know that much about it!"

———— ★ ————

Even on the home front, politicians are not immune to put-downs. Senator Richter took this shot from his lovely wife, Dorothy Jean, a well-known Austin political activist. Having dropped off a suit at a dry cleaner whose shop they did not use routinely, he casually mentioned that fact to D.J., whimsically adding, "I wanted you to know just in case I drop dead before I have a chance to pick it up." She replied, a bit too matter-of-factly, the Senator thought, "If you drop dead, I wouldn't need to pick it up, would I?"

———— ★ ————

Former Land Commissioner Bob Armstrong tells the Adlai Stevenson story about a Democratic convention when Adlai encountered a noticeably pregnant pro-Stevenson delegate. She was carrying a sign with Adlai's campaign slogan, but with a somewhat different implication given her present condition: "Adlai's the Man."

———— ★ ————

Politicians learn to deal with abuse, usually by ignoring it, occasionally by shooting back. Churchill was the classic. At a social engagement, Churchill's bitter foe, the American-born Lady Astor, reacted to a Churchillian aside by saying, "If you were my husband, I would put poison in your coffee." He replied, "Madam, if I were your husband, I'd drink it."

———— ★ ————

Another classic English political story that appears in various forms on the Texas pol circuit is of Gladstone and Disraeli. At one point during a heated exchange, Disraeli roared, "Sir, I predict that you will have a ghastly demise, either on the gallows or from some horrible disease." "That," replied Gladstone, "would depend, I suppose, on whether I embraced your principles or your mistress."

———— ★ ————

Liz Carpenter tells this story about the Texas rawhide candor of the late Maury Maverick, Sr. As the beleaguered Mayor of San Antonio, Maury was accosted one day in the lobby of the St. Anthony Hotel by a pushy lady patriot. "Someone told me the other day that you are a communist, Mr. Maverick," she shrilled, "but I didn't believe them." Whereupon the Mayor drew himself up to his full five feet, two inches, and replied in a similar voice, "Madam, someone told me the other day that you are a whore, but I didn't believe them."

Surviving criticism is the subject of another Mo Udall story. Following a long and eloquent sermon on the importance of fellowship and getting along with one's neighbors, a preacher asked the congregation, "Is there anyone present who has led such a life that he does not have any enemies?"

In the fifth row, an old gentleman, gaunt, gray, and wrinkled, slowly rose from his seat, and in a quavering voice said, "Right here, parson."

"Congratulations," said the preacher. "Please tell the congregation how you did it."

The old man looked around the room, winked, and said, "I outlived the sumbitches!"

Legend has it that Jim Wright once was accosted by a slightly tipsy stranger in a Washington lounge who snarled, "All Texas congressmen are rich, swaggering, uncouth braggarts."

"Simply not true," replied Jim calmly. "We're not all rich."

Sam Rayburn faced a hostile young man one time, and the man angrily accused him of being an old fogey. The reply: "Well, there's one thing worse than being an old fogey, and that's being a young fogey, Mr. Fogey."

———— ★ ————

Speaker Sam was one of a considerable number of our esteemed public servants who have had bald pates and who therefore have endured the occasional gibes of irreverent colleagues and other would-be comedians. Speaker Nicholas Longworth of Ohio presided over the House in the 'Twenties. On one occasion, a colleague playfully passed his hand over Longworth's bald pate and commented, impudently, "Feels just like my wife's bottom." Unabashed, Longworth then passed his own hand over his head and remarked, thoughtfully, "You know, it does, doesn't it?"

———— ★ ————

Despite the abuse from voters and citizens generally, probably no one says worse things about politicians than other politicians — and sometimes by invitation. Political roasts have developed into a fine, though vicious art form. Sitting through one's own roast can be a tough way to raise funds, as shown by some of the examples that follow.

———— ★ ————

Bob Bullock remains one of the most roastable of Texas officeholders. At a Texas Women's Political Caucus benefit, Bullock was the guest of "honor," and naturally, given the beneficiary group, sexist and risque jokes were the order of the day.

———— ★ ————

U.S. Rep. Jake Pickle began by asking why the activist women would honor Comptroller Bob Bullock at all. "He thinks the ERA stands for Elope, Ravage and Annul." Pickle also pointed out that he had just finished helping pass an $8 billion bill for Superfund. "Most of that will go for disposal of Bullock's liver." Pickle continued: "Join me in welcoming one of the best public officials this state has ever sent to California for treatment." Former Lt. Gov. Ben Barnes took an historical view, observing that "this is the first time Bullock and I have been in a room with women when it wasn't raided."

———— ★ ————

Sarah Weddington recalled that, during the campaign season, Bullock had a unique explanation of his own popularity with female voters: "I get along well with women. I've been married five times — and they are supporting me 3 to 2." Lt. Gov. Bill Hobby also focused on Bullock's extensive marital history: "Bullock doesn't have a lot of friends. He does have a lot of ex-wives. He's the only person I know whose marriage license reads 'To whom it may concern.'"

Political cartoon by Ben Sargent. Courtesy of the Austin American Statesman.

———— ★ ————

State Senator Cyndi Taylor Krier referred to the effect of a long speech by Bullock to the Texas Senate, where Krier had been feuding for some time with Senator Carl Parker. "I wouldn't want to say Bullock was boring, but it was the only time Senator Parker and I ever slept together."

————— ★ —————

As usual, Texas Agriculture Commissioner Jim Hightower had some of the best lines. "I have mixed emotions about Bullock. Mixed emotions are when your daughter comes home from the prom with a Gideon Bible." Calling the Comptroller "slicker than bus station chili," Hightower had these comments on Bullock's lengthy record of public service: "Thirty years ago Bob Bullock stuck his snout in the public trough, and he hasn't come up for air since. He also learned the Texas Legislative credo early: If it's worth winnin', it's worth cheatin' for." Hightower concluded by recognizing Bullock's political stature. "You're a big man, Bob, but of course if we took the BS out of you, you'd fit in a matchbox."

————— ★ —————

Even Republican Governor Bill Clements put in a last-minute appearance at the Bullock roast, favorably comparing his and Bullock's mutual strong points. "There are many similarities between myself and Bullock. Our personalities, for example. We're just smiling, happy-go-lucky guys. Bob takes criticism as well as I do. And invariably, as the burns heal and the wounds bind, the critic comes to realize the correctness of Bullock's position."

————— ★ —————

Clements' remarks led someone else to recall Don Regan's statement that "I'm not arrogant. I just believe there's no human problem that can't be solved — if people would simply do as I tell 'em."

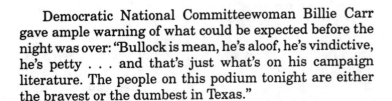

Democratic National Committeewoman Billie Carr gave ample warning of what could be expected before the night was over: "Bullock is mean, he's aloof, he's vindictive, he's petty . . . and that's just what's on his campaign literature. The people on this podium tonight are either the bravest or the dumbest in Texas."

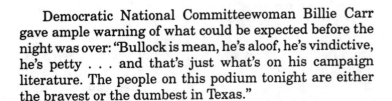

Carr was right. As the program turned to Bullock's reply, he ripped the roasters. He called Caucus members "the worst configuration of deformed feet, sagging bustlines and big bottoms I've ever seen — if an ace bandage on one of you old plugs burst it'd create a chain reaction all the way to China." Turning on roaster Ben Barnes, Bullock reminded the crowd that Barnes officially changed his name from Benny Frank Barnes to Ben; he observed that "if there is one or more female of *any* species in a room, Barnes will be there." Bullock succinctly disposed of roaster Hightower in appropriately agricultural terms: "I just can't look at Jim without thinking about pig droppings." The evening continued like that, and Bullock concluded with this appreciative respect for the female assemblage: "You *have* come a long way. You got minimum wages and careers — I think that's fine. But if you don't pick up anything else here (of course, you can always pick up Barnes), just remember — I loved you when you combed your legs and braided your underarms and I still love you."

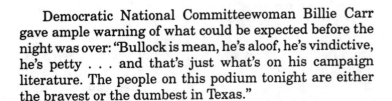

71

Bullock also likes to tell of ribbing W. S. (Bill) Heatly, longtime chairman of the House Appropriations Committee and widely-acclaimed all-around curmudgeon of the Texas Legislature. They had been discussing a range of subjects including the benefits and perks of being state officials. The discussion turned to the right to be buried in the state cemetery in Austin, and Bullock told Heatly that he had seen a map of the cemetery and knew the location of Heatly's reserved grave site.

"Bill," Bullock told the ultra-conservative legislator from Paducah, "they are going to put you between Sissy Farenthold and Sarah Weddington" — two well-known liberal, former lawmakers, and feminist leaders. Fumed Heatly: "Over my dead body, they will."

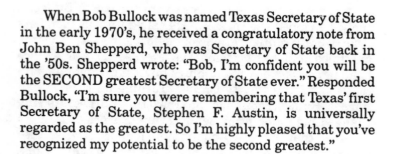

When Bob Bullock was named Texas Secretary of State in the early 1970's, he received a congratulatory note from John Ben Shepperd, who was Secretary of State back in the '50s. Shepperd wrote: "Bob, I'm confident you will be the SECOND greatest Secretary of State ever." Responded Bullock, "I'm sure you were remembering that Texas' first Secretary of State, Stephen F. Austin, is universally regarded as the greatest. So I'm highly pleased that you've recognized my potential to be the second greatest."

At a roasting of State Senator Carlos Truan, area celebrities designated him a "Texas Hysterical Monument." One roaster recalled that when Truan graduated from Texas A & I University, he was awarded a degree that read "Magna Cum Loudmouth," and that "While some guys can talk for hours on a subject, Carlos doesn't even need a subject." Another sympathetically referred to Truan's heart attack. "When Truan was in the hospital, he received tons of hurry up and get well and go home cards from the nurses."

The printed program for an event "honoring" Texas Democratic Party Chairman Bob Slagle offered these opinions about Bob: (1) "If you took all the B. S. out of Bob Slagle, all you'd have left is a little dab of Brylcream and a cigarette holder." (2) "Whenever you need to talk he listens, but sometimes he finishes listening before you finish talking." (3) "His pet parrot died of frustration because it never got a chance to say anything." Other Slagle admirers addressed:

- His conversational skills: "Slagle not only monopolizes a conversation, he also monotonizes it."
- His thorough political knowledge: "If a little knowledge is a dangerous thing, why would anybody be afraid of Bob?"
- The elevated intellectual plane of his political discourse: "He always speaks straight from the shoulder. He'd be more interesting if his thoughts came from a little higher up."

El Pasoans and other friends of State Rep. Nancy McDonald roasted her at a function for the Mental Health Association. The fact that she and her husband Will had 10 children in 13 years drew some attention. For example, her friend Lynne Hodnett declared, "I had been on the mailing list for an organization called Zero Population Growth for ten years, and when they found out that I associated with Nancy, they immediately struck my name from their list."

Chapter Three

Governor Ann Richards added her two cents worth with a videotaped message: "Ten kids in 13 years. The woman had to run for the state legislature just to get out of the house."

──────── ★ ────────

At another event, Ann herself received these gibes from Austin media personality, author, and comedian Cactus Pryor:

- "Ann Richards would save the state $5,000 a year if she'd give up Spray Net."
- "The Texas Rangers had to call ASPCA on Ann when they found out her lap dog was a pit bull."
- "Ann makes Madalyn Murray O'Hair look like Mother Teresa!"

──────── ★ ────────

Molly Ivins tells another Ann Richards' story that shows both Ann's wit and her impatience with small-mindedness and bigotry.

Several years ago there was a big political do at Scholz Beer Garten in Austin and everybody who was anybody in political Texas was there, meetin' and greetin' at a furious pace. About halfway through the evening, a little group of us got the tired feet and went to lean our butts against a table by the back wall of the Garten. Like birds in a row were perched Bob Bullock, the state comptroller; me; Charlie Miles, a black man who was then head of Bullock's personnel department (and the reason Bullock had such a good record in minority hiring); and Ms. Ann Richards. Bullock, having been in Texas politics for thirty some-odd years, consequently knows every living sorry, no-account sumbitch who ever held office. A dreadful old racist judge from East Texas came up to him, "Bob, my boy, how are yew?" The two of them commenced to clap one another on the back and have a big greetin'.

"Judge," said Bullock. "I want you to meet my friends. This is Molly Ivins with the *Texas Observer*."

The judge peered up at me and said, "How yew, little lady?"

"This is Charles Miles, who heads my personnel department." Charlie stuck out his hand and the judge got an expression on his face as though he had just stepped into a fresh cowpie. It took him a long minute before he reached out, barely touched Charlie's hand and said, "How yew, *boy*?" Then he turned with great relief to pretty, blue-eyed Ann Richards and said, "And who is this lovely lady?"

Ann beamed and said, "I am *Mrs.* Miles."

———— ★ ————

In May of 1986 the late Congressman Mickey Leland kicked off a roast of his colleague, Jim Wright, by asserting, "We all know Jim Wright is certain to be the next Speaker of the House; after all, he tells us so every day." At the end, Jim rebutted this by declaring, "People say I spend all my waking hours thinking of becoming Speaker when Tip O'Neill retires at the end of 1986. That is emphatically not true. After all, that election is not going to take place for another six months — (pause) 22 days, 18 hours, and 47 minutes."

———— ★ ————

Apart from roasts, politicians simply enjoy gigging each other, sometimes gently, sometimes not. When Governor Clements swore in Senator J. E. "Buster" Brown as president pro tempore in 1989, the Senator said he felt the responsibility of being third in line for the governorship if anything, "God forbid," should happen to Governor Clements and Lieutenant Governor Bill Hobby. He thanked the two men for their leadership and, as a token of his esteem, said he wanted to give each a present. For the governor, he suggested "two weeks of free sky-diving lessons," and for Hobby, "free bull-fighting lessons."

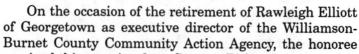

On the occasion of the retirement of Rawleigh Elliott of Georgetown as executive director of the Williamson-Burnet County Community Action Agency, the honoree received this roasting from Senator Richter.

"I'm a bit ashamed since my statement tonight goes against my mother's training. She always declared that if you can't say anything good about someone, it's best not to say anything at all. . . . Something positive I can say is that I'm sure Rawleigh Elliott will live to a ripe old age. I base this on that well-known truism, namely, that THE GOOD DIE YOUNG. Friends, applying that criteria, we can expect this man to live to a hundred and ten.

"I've also heard it said that Rawleigh's honesty and integrity have never been questioned. Hell, I've never even heard them mentioned."

Naturally, exchanges between political opponents tend to include the harshest language of all. From Charles Gore, on his opponent, Speaker (and avid hunter) Gib Lewis: "He's so unethical he probably shoots quail on the ground." Even more pointedly, Jim Hightower said of opponent Rick Perry's misstatements: "If BS was music, my opponent would be the Boston Philharmonic."

Flat-out falsehoods and sheer nonsense are standard fare for political charges. Clayton Williams' spokesman Gordon Hensley made this charge against Ann Richards' insurance reform proposals: "Richards is a political ambulance-chaser. Asking Ann Richards to solve the insurance problem is like asking the Boston Strangler for a neck massage." Once in office, Ann quickly gave lie to the charge, of course, instituting the most aggressive insurance reform efforts in the state's history.

Will Rogers made a comment about Herbert Hoover that still receives substantial circulation, directed against other targets: "It's not what he doesn't know that bothers me; it's what he knows that just ain't so."

In 1983, Congressman Charles Stenholm was roasted after he had already been identified as one of the leading Boll Weevils, the group of conservative Democrats who were supporting many of President Reagan's initiatives. Someone commented that Charlie occasionally still voted with the Democrats; in fact, Speaker Tip O'Neill was so appreciative of his support that he awarded Stenholm a certificate proclaiming him an Honorary Democrat.

Another speaker commented that if Lyndon were there, he'd likely have suggested that Charlie's voting lapses resulted from his having played too much football without a helmet. Stenholm had been a star back for Stamford High School, which may be what prompted the coach at longtime rival Anson High School to say, "The problem with the Stamford team is that they use an unbalanced line, and the backfield isn't even that bright!"

Republican Tom Loeffler, one of Charlie's colleagues in the House at the time, noted that Stenholm had always been a strong foe of bureaucratic red tape. Loeffler gave this example. "You know about those government forms which contain the admonition, DO NOT WRITE IN THIS SPACE? Well, Charlie sent some of those back after scribbling on the form 'I'll write where I damn well please.'"

Some years back, at the unveiling of an official oil painting of Congressman Jack Brooks, Chairman of the House Judiciary Committee, several of his colleagues used the occasion to give Jack a good grilling. A memorable contribution came from then Speaker Jim Wright, who brought forth this original limerick:

> All hail our chairman named Brooks,
> Scourge of wrongdoers and crooks;
>   With withering stare
>   And cigar-chomping glare,
> This guy's just as mean as he looks.

That characterization of Jack — who in fact intimidated strangers with his brusque mannerisms — prompted him to respond defensively, "It's really not true. I've always thought of myself as kind and compassionate, and that's how I want to be remembered."

Like politicians, the term "politics" has received more than its fair share of disparagement. Mao Tse-Tung observed that politics is war without bloodshed and for the most part he was right — usually there's no physical blood. There is, however, plenty of psychological and emotional blood and tears shed in political battles.

On the plus side, Henry Adams was about as positive as it ever gets when he said that politics is the "systematic organization of hatreds."

On the negative side, in a lecture at the University of Texas, John Kenneth Galbraith suggested that modern politics is no longer really the art of the possible, but rather now consists of "choosing between the disastrous and the unpalatable." Speaking of disastrous, *Dallas Morning News* columnist Sam Attlesey quotes another definition of politics: "The art of keeping as many balls as possible up in the air at one time — while protecting your own."

One of the least flattering of all recent definitions was Libertarian Party gubernatorial candidate Theresa Doyle's: "Have you ever examined the word 'politics'? Poly means many and ticks means bloodsuckers."

With all of the apparently inevitable abuse and risk, what's the attraction of politics? Political consultant Bill Miller gave this answer: "Politics is show biz for ugly people." National columnist Jimmie Reston has this explanation: "Politics is like booze and women — dangerous but incomparably exciting." Focusing on the disaster potential, Republican political consultant Rob

Allyn had this explanation for the constant fascination with Texas politics: "Kinda like people slowing down at a wreck on a highway to see the dead."

In part, the fascination of politics lies in its unpredictability. As Jack DeVore, longtime spokesperson for Senator Bentsen, remarked, "Politics is played with a football, not a basketball. It takes real funny bounces."

One longtime political activist asserted that politicians and dogs are alike in several respects: they both get petted a lot, but they get kicked a lot, too; time speeds by for them at about seven times as fast as normal; many things happen to them that they simply don't understand; and, occasionally, they become rabid.

In Texas, state judges are elected, federal judges are appointed. That difference has engendered great controversy through the state's history. Indeed, three times during the state's early years, appointive systems briefly prevailed for state judges, but each time popular outcry forced a change back to allowing voters to make the selections. In either selection system, of course, politics abounds, but the elective system subjects judges to the pleasures, pains, and perhaps most importantly, to the humbling experiences of the campaign trail.

On the other hand, in recent years federal judges have assumed increasing responsibility for "running" Texas government, from prisons to mental health systems to legislative redistricting. Denounced as dictators and demigods — often by the same state legislators whose own inaction and failure to address major state issues have compelled the federal court intervention in the first place — in their more pleasant moments, Texas federal judges have received some good-natured ribbing. One of the best at dishing it out is himself a member of the exalted judicial priesthood, United States District Judge Jerry Buchmeyer. Judge Buchmeyer is so well-recognized as a collector and purveyor of legal humor and anecdotes that the State Bar of Texas enlisted his aid to develop a series of humorous ads for the state's legal profession to try to improve its image.

Buchmeyer describes his own profession's popularity this way: "Federal judges have no real enemies, but they are intensely disliked by their friends." Another Buchmeyer item is directed at the self-centered self importance of some federal judges: "Federal Judge _____ is changing his religion; he no longer believes that he is God."

By contrast, former Chief Justice of the Texas Supreme Court Jack Pope tells two stories illustrating the lessons in humility that a state district judge sometimes learns the hard way. The first occurred when he was sworn in as a district judge in Nueces County in 1946. "I suddenly learned that I was possessed of great wisdom; my anecdotes seemed to be much more amusing to lawyers, too.

"One day, in my wisdom, when the prosecuting attorney was having some trouble with a witness in a case about an assault with a deadly weapon, I thought that I could take over and get quickly to the fact he was seeking to prove. The witness, who had been the victim of an attack and a beating by a man who was hitting him with a rock, was frightened and almost speechless.

"My questioning from on high went something like this. 'Now Arthur, how big was this rock that you say he was beating you with?'

'Well, I know, but I can't tell you in words.'

'Was it as big as my fist?' (showing him my fist).

'It was bigger than that, judge.'

'Was it as big as my two fists?'

'It was bigger than that.'

'Well, Arthur, was it as big as my head?'

'Judge, it was about that big, but not that thick.'

"That was the day, early in my career, that I learned that a judge speaks through silence and solemn judgment."

Justice Pope's second story relates an experience he had just after he had run for and been elected to the Court of Civil Appeals in 1950, at age 37.

"Chief Justice W. O. Murray, Justice James Norvell, and I constituted the court. About four months after I had taken the bench, a seasoned lawyer from down in what we called the brush country, appeared to argue his case.

"The opening remarks and comments went about like this: 'Your honors, I tried this case before a judge down in my county who had been on the bench only for 90 days. He will one day, I'm sure, become a very good judge, but his lack of experience caused him to make every kind of error you can imagine and my client did not get a fair trial.'

"Pope: 'Counsel, I think it is only fair that I tell you that I have been an appellate judge for only about 120 days, myself.'

"Counsel: 'Judge, 30 days can make an awful lot of difference.'"

Back to Judge Buchmeyer on the federal bench: "How many federal judges does it take to change a lightbulb? Only one. He just holds onto the bulb — and the universe revolves around him."

Federal judges hold office "during good behavior," which as a practical matter means life tenure. Some lawyers have argued that Texas should adopt a version of the so-called Missouri Plan, under which judges run for reelection, but without an opponent. Under that system, of course, a judge's reelection is virtually automatic. (In Missouri itself, voters have been able to remove only one judge in over 50 years under that system.) Former Texas Supreme Court Justice Franklin Spears quoted an Arizona reporter's description of reelection prospects under the similar system followed in that state. "Short of committing incest at high noon at Central and Van Buren, it would appear that our honorable judges now have lifetime sinecures."

Or as famed West Texas trial lawyer Warren Burnett similarly explained: "In political combat, as in speed contests among horses, the outcome becomes doubtful only after the entry of the second contestant." George Ade phrased a similar political adage, "Anybody can win, unless there happens to be a second entry."

Proponents of the elective system are fond of pointing out that selecting judges by appointment "doesn't take politics out of the system, it takes the voters out of the system." The lobbying engaged in by judicial office seekers and their supporters when a midterm vacancy comes open for gubernatorial appointment is intense. Shortly after Republican Governor Bill Clements had been accused of participating in a scheme to pay football players at SMU, he announced his support for an appointed judiciary. Rejoined Justice William Kilgarlin: "Is he going to try to reform the court like he did the SMU Athletic Department?"

What does it take to make a good judge? Again, judicial jester Buchmeyer has collected some of the best formulations:

- "Chief Justice John Marshall once said it was the ability 'to look a lawyer straight in the face for two solid hours and not hear a damn word he says.'"
- "How can you be a good judge? I've learned you've got to do it every day. One day of being a good judge is like one day of clean living. It just ain't gonna help."
- "Being a good judge is not that hard. The secret is to act as if you've known all of your life what you just learned five minutes ago.'"

Good judges sometimes must be like good parents: understanding. Mo Udall tells this story about a Texas judge. A disreputable fellow in a small town was sentenced to thirty days for stealing a ham. Two weeks after he had begun the sentence, his wife visited the judge to beg for his release.

"Is he a good husband?" the judge asked.

"No, sir, he's a no-account."

"Does he treat the children well?"

"No, sir, he's right mean to them."

"Well, does he stay at home when he's not in jail?"

"No, sir, he runs around a lot." "Then," asked the judge, "why in the world do you want him out of jail?"

"I'll tell you, judge," the woman said, "we're about to run out of ham."

———— ★ ————

Another understanding judge with a common touch is U.S. Fifth Circuit Court of Appeals Judge Reynaldo Garza from Brownsville. Once when he was a trial judge, the federal government brought criminal charges in his court against two farmers who, by mistake, had mislabeled some of their cotton in violation of some technical regulation. The government brought all of its majestic weight crashing down upon the backs of the simple farmers, who were too poor to hire lawyers. The prosecution team had four lawyers, one from the U.S. Department of Agriculture in Washington, another from the regional USDA office, still another from the Justice Department, and the local Assistant U.S. Attorney. After a two-day bench trial, the evidence concluded, and Judge Garza announced his judgment: "I find that the Government has proved its case, and indeed has proved it overwhelmingly. The defendants, these farmers, are clearly guilty. They are clearly guilty of what is a very technical violation of a very technical regulation. I also find that this case never should have been brought in the first place by the government. It's a waste of time and money. This is a two-bit case and a two-bit prosecution. I therefore find the defendants guilty and I assess the punishment as a fine in the amount of two bits."

———— ★ ————

Former Texas Supreme Court Chief Justice Jack Pope also has a two-bit item. Friends of former Attorney General R. L. Bobbitt enjoyed kidding him about his renowned frugality. One of their best gigs was to quote the shoe shine man at the Driskill Hotel: "Mr. Bobbitt is the most courageous man I ever knew. He is one man who gives no quarter."

———— ★ ————

Moving up to six-bit words, in Latin no less, Odessa lawyer Warren Burnett tells of a time when he argued to the U.S. Fifth Circuit Court of Appeals in New Orleans. A learned and erudite judge on the appellate panel interrupted Burnett's oral argument at one point to ask him, "Mr. Burnett, I suggest that this case is controlled by the principle of 'Res inter alios acta.' Are you familiar with that doctrine?"

With his usual aplomb, Burnett responded immediately, "Why, your Honor, in Odessa, Texas, where I come from, the people speak of little else."

——————— ★ ———————

Former Texas Supreme Court Justice William Kilgarlin recited these instructions from his friend Tom Stovall on how to become an adviser to the very highest levels of government: "One day Stovall proclaimed 'I have now become one of the Governor's advisers.' He explained 'Just yesterday the Governor told me "Stovall, if I want your advice, I will ask for it."

——————— ★ ———————

Another item of judicial advice goes back to El Paso Judge Woodrow Bean, a genuine all-time colorful character. The hard-drinking judge once underwent a serious piece of stomach surgery. Afterwards, the doctor told him, "Judge, the best thing for you to do is to give up the booze."

Whereupon Woody replied, "Doc, I've been such a reprobate, I don't deserve the best. What's the second best?"

——————— ★ ———————

Also from West Texas comes this item from federal Judge Lucius Bunton, who tells of the prospective juror who completed the standard juror questionnaire form. In the blank labeled "Sex _____," the juror simply wrote in "twice."

———— ★ ————

At last count, 59 members of the Texas Legislature were lawyers, so we'll end this chapter with just a few choice shots by deadeye Judge Buchmeyer against some of the fattest targets of all, Texas lawyers:

- Why should lawyers be substituted in laboratory experiments in place of white mice? (1) Lawyers are not as messy as white mice. (2) There are more lawyers than white mice. (3) You don't get personally attached to lawyers. (4) There are some things that white mice just won't do.
- What do you need when you find three lawyers buried up to their necks in sand? More sand!
- What do you call 500 dead lawyers at the bottom of the ocean? A good start!
- Why does New Jersey have more toxic waste dumps while Texas has more lawyers? New Jersey got first choice.
- What's the best way to save a marriage? Talk about fees with a few divorce lawyers.
- What is a criminal lawyer? Redundant.
- What's the difference between a lawyer and a bucket of manure? The bucket.

CHAPTER FOUR

The Lege

The Texas Legislature is often entertaining, often abysmally unenlightened, and on very, very rare occasion, inspiring. Fortunately, the Legislature generates substantial quantities of humorous material, albeit much of it by accident.

English editor Walter Bagehot said that the cure for admiring the House of Lords "is to go and look at it." The same can be said of the Texas Legislature. Representative Fred Hill observed a kiddie Easter-egg hunt in the House chamber one day, and commented, "This is a whole lot like when the Legislature is in session. The only difference is that today we have adult supervision."

But it is entertaining. Representative Wilhelmina Delco of Austin once introduced the opening production of a play at Austin's Capitol City Playhouse. "I am not much of a theater-goer," she said. "I don't have the time. I do go to the real theater, however, which we call the Texas Legislature."

When Ann Richards was State Treasurer, she was a hit as mistress of ceremonies at an annual Chamber of Commerce banquet in Austin. She said a reporter had asked her what should be on the top of the Capitol during the restoration of the Goddess of Liberty. "I like the Christmas star," she replied. "Maybe it will attract some wise men." A Christmas star was indeed mounted on top of the Capitol; there's no significant evidence that her other hope was fulfilled.

Unquestionably the most outstanding humorist/chronicler of legislative folly in the state's history is Molly

Ivins. No one has a keener eye for the absurd, nor a sharper tongue to tell about it. In her best-selling book, *Molly Ivins Can't Say That, Can She?*, Molly pointed out that in 1971 the Citizens Conference on State Legislatures wrote a comparative study entitled "The Sometime Governments," and ranked the Texas Legislature 38th out of the 50. That result, Molly said, led to "stunned reactions among connoisseurs of the local peculiar institution, such as, 'My God! You mean there are twelve worse than this?'"

Perennially youthful wit though she is, Molly has lamented the decline of legislative unruliness, pointing out that the last "all-House duke-out" was over ten years ago. Her vivid description of the last governmental pro-wrestling event was magnificent:

> Although there have been a fair number of fistfights in the Capitol since, none has qualified as total Fist City. On the last such occasion (the cause long forgotten), over half of the 150 House members were actively engaged in slugging their colleagues, insulting the wives and mothers of same, knocking over desks, and throwing chairs. Now any legislature can have a mass duke-out, but where else would there be musical accompaniment? In mid-melee, four members mounted the speaker's dais and held forth, in barbershop-quartet harmony, with "I Had a Dream, Dear."

Over the years, such events have engendered not a small measure of understandable skepticism on the part of the Texas citizenry. The story is told of a man who had taken his young son up into the Texas Senate gallery to watch the proceedings. The young man, noting that a speaker had stepped up to the podium as the session was about to convene, asked his father, "Who's that?"

Father replied, "That's the Senate chaplain; he's going to give a prayer to open the session."

"Is he going to pray for the senators?" asked the boy.

After a thoughtful pause, the father answered: "No, son. He'll look out over that body of senators and then he'll pray for the State of Texas."

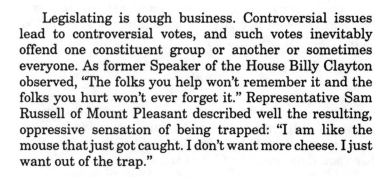

Legislating is tough business. Controversial issues lead to controversial votes, and such votes inevitably offend one constituent group or another or sometimes everyone. As former Speaker of the House Billy Clayton observed, "The folks you help won't remember it and the folks you hurt won't ever forget it." Representative Sam Russell of Mount Pleasant described well the resulting, oppressive sensation of being trapped: "I am like the mouse that just got caught. I don't want more cheese. I just want out of the trap."

How to explain the tough vote? There has never been a keener observer of legislative goings-on, nor a funnier pundit, than former legislator and Texas Land Commissioner Bob Armstrong, who relates this story about Texas Congressman Joe Pool. Congressman Mo Udall had sponsored and was working for the passage of the National Wilderness Act, and Pool came to talk to him. Pool asked: "What are you talking about in this legislation?"

Udall explained the legislation at some length and then Pool inquired "Do you need my vote?" Udall said that he probably did not; passage looked fairly certain.

Pool then asked, "Is LBJ for it?" Udall said that LBJ was for it, that it was a key element in his national environmental program and that Lady Bird was also strongly behind the legislation. Pool said that because LBJ was fairly unpopular in his own district, he would probably vote against it. The vote came out 423 to 1 in favor of the legislation.

The one vote was Joe Pool. The *Dallas Morning News*, *Dallas Times Herald*, and many other papers immediately called Pool to find out why he opposed this overwhelmingly popular legislation. Pool called Udall and pleaded, "What do I tell them, how in the world can I explain this?"

Udall said: "You've got only one chance. Tell them that you voted against the legislation as a protest, because you think there was not enough wilderness land included in it."

With tongue twisted in cheek, former Lieutenant Governor Bill Hobby created an interesting vote call in connection with a bill in 1986 to change San Jacinto Day to a special recognition of 150 years of Texas independence: "All in favor say aye; all opposed say Sesquicentennial."

At a meeting of the House Insurance Committee, Representative Mike Martin expressed the almost system-wide dysfunction that afflicts a lawmaking body consisting mostly of lawyers. He asked insurance company lobbyists to explain the statistics on rates that they had cited: "Statistics are very difficult for me because I can't add or multiply. Somewhere in my life I lost the ability to do that; that's why I am a lawyer."

One need listen to very little legislative debate to be thoroughly convinced of the accuracy of Louis Brandeis' maxim that, "Behind every argument is someone's ignorance." Debate is the stuff of formal legislative discourse, though, and as Lieutenant Governor Bob Bullock said, "Any time two friends agree on everything, one of them is unnecessary."

GOVERNMENT BY DECREE.

GOVERNMENT BY CONSENT.

GOVERNMENT BY CUISINART.

★

Former Chief Justice of the Texas Supreme Court, Bob Calvert, who also was a former Speaker of the House, recalled the occasion when "two of our less brilliant" representatives were arguing about the merits of a particular bill. One said to the other, "Why are you trying to tell me about this bill? You never got out of the third grade."

The other replied, "If I hadn't went to school at all, I'd have more sense than you've got."

At this juncture, Calvert recalls, "The smart young representative from Decatur, Herman Jones (later to become a distinguished jurist), arose at his desk, sought and obtained recognition by the Speaker by shouting, 'Point of order, Mr. Speaker. Point of order.'"

The Speaker replied: "State your point of order, Mr. Jones."

Mr. Jones: "Mr. Speaker, I raise a point of order that this is a battle of wits and both parties are unarmed."

Chapter Four

———— ★ ————

Similarly, during the 1991 Regular Session, Representative Eddie Cavazos was arguing with a colleague who accused Eddie of breaking an agreement. The member declared that there had been "a meeting of the minds." Cavazos angrily shot back, "There may have been a meeting, but my mind wasn't invited!"

———— ★ ————

Representative Doyle Willis recalls the time that Carl Parker, a colleague of Willis's at the time, was helping him with a firemen and policemen rights bill by explaining a certain section of the measure. Representative Ray Hutchison got on the back mike and started asking Parker questions which Parker answered. Ray kept repeating a certain question, and Carl kept giving him the same answer. Finally, Doyle remembers, Parker became exasperated and shouted at Hutchison, "Listen, Mr. Hutchison, I can explain the bill for you BUT I CAN'T UNDERSTAND IT FOR YOU!"

———— ★ ————

Debates can get ugly, and as utility public advocate Kingsberry Ottmers indicated, often the most sensible tactic is to withdraw from the battlefield, or as the case may be, the pigpen: "You don't mud-wrestle with a pig. You just get all dirty, and the pig loves it." Representative Doyle Willis once explained his not arguing with Republicans about redistricting: "I would have been about as successful as a Siamese cat getting in with ten pit bulldogs."

———— ★ ————

Bitter floor fights are the best cure for paranoia: "You find out that you have real enemies," declared one representative. Indeed, Representative M. A. Taylor once proclaimed that the rotunda in the State Capitol was round because the architect figured that legislators needed at least one place in the Capitol where they could not be cornered.

Perhaps the best use of humor on the floor is to make a point. Former Senator Babe Schwartz, a white-maned elf from Galveston, was a master at this. He scored telling points against a proposed version of a new constitution with the following story, related by Molly Ivins: "Fellow delegates, this new constitution they are offering us for a vote today reminds me of the time the seeing-eye dog peed on his master's leg. The blind man stood still for a moment and then reached into his pocket for a doggie biscuit. He fished out the biscuit and leaned down and gave it to the dog. And when the dog took it, he patted its head. A bystander observed this and was most touched. 'Why, sir,' he said to the blind man, 'I see you've given that dog a biscuit even though he peed on your leg. You clearly recognize how much you depend on that dog, how much he does for you even though he's made this mistake, and you are treating him kindly anyway. Sir, that's wonderful.'

"And the blind man said, 'Listen, you jackleg, I gave the damn dog the biscuit so I could figure out where his head is so I can kick the hmm-hmm out of his tail, and that's just what I'm fixing to do.'

"Gentlemen, I suggest to you that you are being offered a doggie biscuit today, and if you're dumb enough to take it, you know what they're fixing to do."

Well-known for his verbal stamina, Senator Schwartz one day addressed the chair: "Mr. President, can I speak briefly on this issue?" Whereupon the presiding officer, Lieutenant Governor Bill Hobby replied, "Yes, you MAY speak briefly on this issue, but I doubt that you CAN."

———— ★ ————

On learning that the City of Austin had negotiated to buy electric power generated from West Texas feedlot residue, Jim Hightower noted the directional implications for Texas political discourse: "For the first time in history, BS is going to flow from the countryside into the state capitol."

———— ★ ————

Debate tricks are certainly not unknown on the House floor, and Representative Doyle Willis told of a practical joke his brother Rep. Phil Willis and Rep. Wayne Wagonseller played on another legislator, who was a former Judge from West Texas, during the debate on a controversial piece of legislation. The Judge was noted for his fascination with beautiful women, and on this occasion his two mischievous colleagues spotted an unusually lovely creature in a yellow dress sitting in the House gallery.

They went forthwith to the Judge and told him the lady in the yellow dress was from his district and had come to Austin to hear him make a speech.

This prompted the West Texan to approach the Speaker and ask to speak for the bill. The Speaker told him that only three members could speak FOR and three AGAINST the bill and three members had already signed on to speak for the bill.

The old fellow took another look at the lovely woman in the gallery and said, "Mr. Speaker, I simply have to speak on this bill; it is very important that I do. Just put me down to speak against it." The Speaker did and the Judge did.

Naturally, the beauty in the yellow dress was not from the Judge's district and did not even know him. What's certain, relates Doyle Willis, is that Phil Willis and Wayne Wagonseller got a big kick out of watching the old Judge waving at the girl in the yellow dress — with no response.

During another debate, a bill pending in the Senate would have created a delay between the time of marriage license purchase and the marriage. Senator Chet Edwards remarked in opposition: "If I ever find a woman willing to marry an Aggie politician, I don't want to give her a chance to change her mind."

This provoked Senator Carl Parker, who was fresh from having been battered by the press for an insensitive joke about AIDS victims. Addressing the Press Table, he said, "If you SOBs (meaning the Press) insist that we practice safe humor, Edwards is the best you're going to get."

The Parker wit surfaced on another occasion when a Senate Finance Committee debate was disrupted by Senator Bill Sims' sudden awareness that a colleague, Senator Tati Santiesteban, was crawling around on his hands and knees under the committee table.

"Don't anybody move," shouted Sims. "A colleague has lost a contact lens."

Which prompted Senator Carl Parker to observe, "People in politics search for contacts everywhere."

———— ★ ————

Taxes and budgets are the fundamental stuff of legislative work, but both can be hazardous to a legislator's life expectancy. Long ago, Louis XIV's finance minister, Jean Baptiste Colbert, observed that "The art of taxation consists in so plucking the goose as to obtain the largest amount of feathers with the least amount of hissing." Senator Chet Brooks of Pasadena, translated that into East Texan: "Proposing taxes at any time is kind of like milking an alligator — fraught with danger at both ends." Or as former Representative Stan Schlueter of Killeen commented on a particularly stout tax bill: "It is going to be like drinking picante sauce straight out of the bottle."

———— ★ ————

As the Texas oil and gas economy has declined, so have the state's revenue sources. Speaker Gib Lewis expressed well the limited potential of ever-increasing taxes on liquor and cigarettes: "With the state looking at sin tax and the federal government looking at sin tax, and those sinners starting to be less sinful, that revenue is decreasing each year." Speaker Gib was famous, or grammatically infamous, for another statement about the sin tax. A teacher publicly challenged Gib's consistently bad "syntax," and received this response: "What 'sin tax'? I'm not for any sin tax. I'm against all new taxes."

———— ★ ————

Another traditional crack directed to this process is that "If the American revolutionaries thought that taxation without representation was bad, they should have seen it with representation."

———— ★ ————

Raising the money is legislatively excruciating, but spending the money and drafting a budget also is hard work. Likewise, cutting a budget — that is, cutting off at least the fingers and toes of one's own constituents — is rugged duty.

Senator Carl Parker, asked to describe the serious financial challenge facing the Legislature in 1989, had this drollery:

"The first thing that came to my mind was that it's like trying to undertake the feeding of 5,000 people with two loaves and five fishes. But I'm afraid we don't have that kind of leadership available.

"And furthermore, let's not forget what happened to the fellow who did that before."

Once when Senator Parker's wife, Beverly, was laboring under the pressure of final preparations for their daughter's wedding, the Senator remarked that his wife had been overcome with the magnitude of this undertaking. In fact, he had told her, "the invasion of Normandy took less time to execute." Maybe so, she agreed, but added, "That involved fewer people and a larger budget."

Ann Richards, then Treasurer of Texas, described the lean diet resulting from a tax shortfall: "Turkey feathers and deer tracks make mighty thin soup."

Spending a little sometimes leads to spending a lot. Former State Representative Maury Maverick, Jr., told of the time President Teddy Roosevelt asked Congress for $1 million to send the fleet to Hong Kong to show the colors. Congress, however, provided TR with only half a million. TR used the money to send the fleet to Hong Kong anyway, and then he sent word to Congress: "It's up to you to get it back."

Tom Craddick, a Republican from Midland simplified his budget priorities to the most fundamental: "If you can't eat it, you don't need it." Representative Doyle Willis put a more rural twist on his needs test in challenging the necessity of the state's grant-seeking office in Washington, D.C.: "It's about as needed as a fifth teat on a West Texas cow."

During the 1991 session, State Comptroller John Sharp conducted a series of rigorous agency audits, resulting in proposals for deep budget cuts. Predictably, reactions were intense, and in some instances, colorful. Representative David Counts of Knox City said, "It's kind of like drinking out of a spittoon — if you've got to do it, do it in one gulp."

Senator Mike Moncrief of Fort Worth commented on the certain prospect of state agency opposition to the reorganization plans: "We don't have a sacred cow down here, we have the whole damn sacred herd." Sunset Commission Director Bill Wells also gleefully anticipated the reaction to the proposed budget cuts: "[Sharp's] got such a herd of sacred cows inside that fence, watch out when the stampede starts." Sharp himself had a similarly bovine rationale for his plan: "I think taxpayers are sick and tired of high-paid bureaucrats and politicians who have a handful of gimme and a mouthful of bull."

Another legislator at the time quoted this aged truism about bureaucracies: "Bureaucracy defends the status quo long past the time when the quo has lost its status."

Deputy Comptroller Billy Hamilton predicted the House's dismemberment of the Sharp revenue proposals: "You've got to remember, Moses only delivered the Ten Commandments; he didn't say you had to keep them."

Budget-cutting can mean trade-offs, and Representative Ted Kamel remarked on that process, "If you rob Peter to pay Paul, you can always count on the support of Paul."

Legislators like to talk about budget-cutting more than they like to cut budgets, a fact Comptroller Sharp highlighted with this analogy. "Everyone wants to cut spending, but not in their own districts. It's kind of like everyone wants to go to heaven but no one wants to die to get there."

Budget "cuttees" tend to react with some vigor. In 1986, Governor Mark White addressed a special session of the Texas Legislature that had convened to deal with the severe budget crisis, and he recounted a warning in the form of a story from another state that "solved" its crisis by laying off employees. One state employee who received notice that he was being laid off was a drawbridge operator. As soon as he got word, he called the Governor by phone. "Sir," he said, "I certainly understand that you've got to let some people go, but I have one question: Do you want me to leave the drawbridge up or down?"

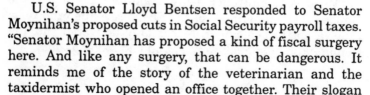

U.S. Senator Lloyd Bentsen responded to Senator Moynihan's proposed cuts in Social Security payroll taxes. "Senator Moynihan has proposed a kind of fiscal surgery here. And like any surgery, that can be dangerous. It reminds me of the story of the veterinarian and the taxidermist who opened an office together. Their slogan was: EITHER WAY YOU GET YOUR DOG BACK." Bentsen concluded: "I want to make sure that when our dogs come home, they're still wagging their tails."

In Texas, legislators, and presumably their constituents, have an unusual attraction to spending money on building prisons. Representative Allen Hightower had this comment on plans to build 30,000 new prison beds: "I have a *Field of Dreams* philosophy about building prisons. If you build them, people will come." Molly Ivins quipped that Texas and California "are running about even to see which state can put the most human beings in Stripe City."

Much of the prison building resulted from federal court orders, some of which have conflicted with each other, prompting this remark from Representative Mark Stiles:

"What we need is a one-armed federal judge who can't say 'on the other hand'."

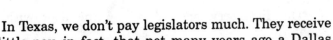

In Texas, we don't pay legislators much. They receive so little pay, in fact, that not many years ago a Dallas representative successfully applied for food stamps while receiving his legislative pay.

At one time, when legislators were receiving about $340 a month take home pay, Governor Bill Clements opposed any pay raise and observed, "Some people think they are overpaid now." At the time, Clements earned $91,600 a year. Someone pointed out the substantial disparity, and Clements magnanimously responded: "And I hope that gap gets wider." Molly Ivins recalls Representative Keith Oakley responded:

> In an effort to narrow the gap one way if not another, Representative Keith Oakley promptly introduced a bill to cut the governor's salary by $84,000 a year. Said Oakley, "He's sitting there saying, 'I think legislators are overpaid,' and he's drawing $92,000 a year and wearing a plaid jacket and going to Taos, New Mexico, all the time and slapping us in the face like that." It is embarrassing to have a governor who wears a plaid jacket all the time.

Though paid little, Texas legislators do have staffs, which can lead to other problems. Congressman Ralph Hall recounted a telephone conversation, during his days as state senator, between a caller and an aide who answered the telephone in the Senator's third floor office. "May I talk to the Senator?" the caller asked. "I'm sorry, the Senator is down on the floor."

"Well, in that case, let me talk to the Senator's secretary."

"Oh, I'm sorry, she's down on the floor with the Senator."

Mary Jane Wardlow, now Assistant Press Secretary to Lt. Gov. Bob Bullock, recalls another telephone faux pas that involved a call by then Secretary of State (Republican) Jack Rains. Mary Jane was working for Bullock, who at the time was State Comptroller.

> As a young Bullock staffer in 1987, I answered my private line one morning with the standard "Tax Information, this is Mary Jane."
>
> A gruff male voice on the other end said, "This isn't the Secretary of State's Office?" "No, Sir," I answered, "this is the Comptroller's . . . ."
>
> Interrupting me, he again demanded, "This ISN'T the Secretary of State's Office?" "No, Sir," I said emphatically, "you have the State Comptroller's Office, but if you'll hang on just a second I'll give you the Secretary of State's main number."
>
> Clearly agitated, the man said "I don't need the number, I have it. I AM the Secretary of State."
>
> Certain I was dealing with a prankster or a lunatic, I looked down silently at my phone display. "Rains, Jack for Wardlow, Mary" I read, just as the politician in him took over and he added, "I'm sorry, I guess I've got people in this office who can't take down a number — but it was real nice talking to you anyway."

———— ★ ————

Not surprisingly, the nonexistent financial rewards of legislative officeholding have contributed to lobby influence and power. Representative Ron Lewis of Mauriceville gave this not overly-persuasive rationale for accepting a lobby-financed ski trip: "We get $600 a month for this job. If you take away my golfings, if you take away my outings, my hunting trips, then what's fun about this job anymore? We don't get paid any money, so that's one of the things about this job that's fun." Former Republican Representative Terral Smith managed to equate burgers and junkets: "I don't see a bit of difference between letting someone fly you to Colorado to discuss legislation, and then skiing for a while, and someone taking you to lunch at Arby's."

———— ★ ————

Smith also teased a representative of Public Citizen, Tom (Smitty) Smith, who had criticized the lack of strong ethics legislation in Texas. "I think Smitty is a tool of the lobby — saying those things just to save them money."

———— ★ ————

Molly Ivins has captured better than anyone else the essence of the traditional legislator-lobbyist relationship in Texas:

> Texas politicians aren't crooks: it's just that they tend to have an overdeveloped sense of the extenuatin' circumstance. As they say around the Legislature, if you can't drink their whiskey, screw their women, take their money, and vote against 'em anyway, you don't belong in office.

———— ★ ————

Molly followed that with a favorite Lubbock political story: "Sometime after Franklin Roosevelt died and before Swatch watches, Lubbock elected a state senator who proceeded to Austin, where he holed up in the Driskill Ho-tell with another senator-elect; they's drinkin' whiskey and 'interviewin' secretaries.' Comes a knock-knock-knock on the door and there's the lobbyist for the chiropractors; he offers 'em each $200 to vote for the chiropractor bill. Guy from Lubbock takes the money. Damn ol' bill comes up first week of the session. Guy from Lubbock votes against it. Hacks off the chiropractor lobbyist something serious.

"'You take my money and you vote against me!' he says.

"Guy from Lubbock says, 'Yeah, but the doctors offered me $400 to vote against you.'

"Now the lobbyist is some pissed. He cusses the senator up one side and down the other. Senator finally gets to feeling resentful. He explains, 'Yeah, but you knew I was weak when I took the $200.'"

Lobby meal tickets used to be standard operating procedure at the legislature, and some new members took advantage of such dining opportunities to increase their epicurean sophistication. Former Representative Jake Johnson enjoyed gigging a former legislative colleague who received a complimentary pass from the Texas Restaurant Association and invited Jake to dine at one of Austin's finest restaurants.

When the waitress brought the host the wine list, he looked it over and seemed puzzled, so he asked her if they had some really fine wine that was not on the list. She asked, "Like what?" He said, "Well, like Mogan David."

How to deal with all that lobby food? Here were Senator Mike Moncrief's two dietary rules: (1) If no one sees you eat it, it contains no calories. (2) If you fatten up everyone else around you, then you look thinner.

On the subject of eating, sort of, the progressive journal the *Texas Observer* paid this "compliment" to then Representative Jim Nugent, now Texas Railroad Commissioner, on a session-long performance combining the best elements of "Dracula, the King of the Nazgul and the Eggplant That Ate Chicago."

The feeding is a two-way deal, of course, and one lobbyist gave this advice to colleagues who received requests for campaign-related favors from legislators who vote against the lobby's interest: "Don't feed the hand that bites you."

Bob Bullock was on both the receiving and sending ends of a food fight. As newly elected State Comptroller, he shut down a Gregg County restaurant for failing to send in the sales tax money collected from its customers. The restaurant shut down while the owner raised the money to pay the delinquent taxes, but then it reopened. Bullock received a special invitation to the grand opening with a pointed reference to a new item on the menu: "Bullock Burgers — Cheap, Tasteless, and Full of Bull!"

Bullock responded in kind: "While I cannot attend the grand opening, I am sure the new Bullock Burgers will be a hot item, just as hot as those dozen hot checks you sent me."

———— ★ ————

Where there's food, there's usually drink, and that combination is certainly another legislative tradition, though less in vogue now than in years past. State Senator Ron Clower of Garland, for example, liked to quote the old legislative rule: "Vote conservative, party liberal." Lyndon Johnson, legislatively raised at the elbow of bourbon drinking "Mr. Sam" Rayburn, would tell this tale about the attractions of drink.

> This story occurred down in my own hills of Texas. When one of our elder statesmen found difficulty in his hearing, he went to the doctor. The doctor examined him carefully and said "How much are you drinking these days?" And he said well he drank about a pint a day.
>
> And the doctor said "Well, if you want to improve your hearing you are going to have to cut out your drinking."
>
> About 90 days later, the fellow went back to the doctor and the doctor examined him again and his hearing hadn't improved a bit. And he asked, "Well now have you cut out your drinking?"
>
> The fellow said "No."
>
> "The doctor upbraided the man, saying, 'Well, I can't do anything for you if you won't follow my advice, take my prescription. Didn't I tell you when you were here that you should cut out your drinking if you wanted to improve your hearing?'
>
> "Yes."
>
> "Well, why didn't you do it?"

"Well, doctor," the man concluded, "I got home and I considered it and I just decided that I liked what I drank so much better than what I heard."

———————— ★ ————————

Johnson also enjoyed Mr. Sam's line about the siren call of drink. "Why be stupid and weak when, with one drink, you can feel smart and strong?"

———————— ★ ————————

Former Senator Joe Christie recalls these words of wisdom by colorful Senator V. E. "Red" Berry, giving the secret to his long life: "Keep your mind sharp by playing poker, and it don't hurt none to drink a little whiskey." (Red also had this response to a preacher's attack on his gambling habits: "I am a retired sinner, but I do come out of retirement now and then.")

———————— ★ ————————

Usually, of course, drinking makes you not-so-smart. Fred Schmidt, former secretary-treasurer of the Texas AFL-CIO and later lecturer at UCLA, recounted a story involving Ted Youngblood, a black man who at one time was head waiter at the Driskill Hotel in Austin. Fred described Youngblood as "every bit as stately as that ancient hotel itself."

This particular episode occurred during the mid-'50s when many Texas politicos were sounding off about how they were going to block integration. In fact, nine bills had been introduced in the legislature to accomplish just that. The setting was a banquet where anti-integration rhetoric flowed freely.

Quoting Schmidt: "A state senator with a bourbon-enhanced voice was giving out his views on racial integration when he looked up into Youngblood's face as he was being served his dessert. Stuck in mid-sentence the senator, a bit abashed, recovered enough to ask, 'What do you think about that, Youngblood?'

The dignified man simply replied, "I'd rather not say, sir. I got family on both sides of that issue."

Helping the lobby sometimes involves simply helping friends. Lobbyist Jake Johnson told this story about obtaining the assistance of Houston Senator Babe Schwartz.

"Twelve years ago I was trying to buy two small city lots on the East side of Houston next to a bank that I had an interest in for additional parking. The taxes had not been paid on the lots for over 20 years and the title was fouled up. I asked Babe Schwartz to carry a bill that would allow the County Tax Assessor to sell real property when the taxes had not been paid over 10 years upon proper notice with public competitive bids without the necessity of going through court.

"A newspaper reporter asked Schwartz why he was carrying the bill. Schwartz told him that his friend Jake Johnson asked him to. The reporter replied that that seemed to go against his principles. Schwartz said, 'Yeah, but sometimes you got to rise above principles to support your friends.'"

State Senator Bill ("Bull of the Brazos") Moore raised this self defense to a charge that he had a personal profit interest in a bill he was supporting: "I'd just make a little bit of money, I wouldn't make a whole lot." Another of Moore's inimitable lines during a heated debate was this comment comparing his source of income to another senator's: "Senator, you married into all your money, but every dime I have was earned right here on the floor of the Senate."

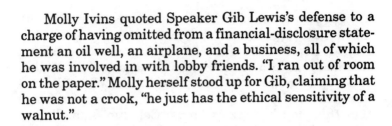

Molly Ivins quoted Speaker Gib Lewis's defense to a charge of having omitted from a financial-disclosure statement an oil well, an airplane, and a business, all of which he was involved in with lobby friends. "I ran out of room on the paper." Molly herself stood up for Gib, claiming that he was not a crook, "he just has the ethical sensitivity of a walnut."

———— ★ ————

The possibly apocryphal story is told of Congressman Charlie Wilson, who supposedly garnered a position on the House Ethics Committee by observing to Mo Udall, as he studied the list of members, "Damn, there is not a son-of-a-bitch on here who likes women or whiskey. They are not representative of the Democratic Caucus."

———— ★ ————

One of the oddest gifts to an officeholder came to Ann Richards from a West Texas admirer(?), who sent her a road-kill raccoon's penis, polished and suitable for a necklace. Ann's press secretary (and general raconteur) Bill Cryer responded with appropriate solemnity to an inquiry concerning how to report the contribution: "It probably didn't have a whole lot of value for reporting purposes. It meant more to the raccoon."

———— ★ ————

Talking ethics is different from doing ethics, and Senator Bill Sims of San Angelo once critiqued a colleague's struggle with ethics reform by noting: "He's a lot like the weather in West Texas — thunders a lot but never rains."

———— ★ ————

The perception of corruption or at least moral frailty among the legislature does not inspire great public respect. Rep. Dan Kubiak tells about a committee meeting that had gone into the wee hours. A tall gray-haired fellow stood up to address the weary legislators. When the witness affirmation was passed around, one member noted that this man had signed in as "Col. Jim Blane," so he proceeded to question him. "I see you signed your affirmation as Colonel. Would you mind telling us about your military career?"

"What do you mean, my military career?"

"Well, if you are a Colonel, isn't it fair for us to assume you had a distinguished military background?"

"Oh, that Colonel, you might say that's like the Honorable in front of YOUR name; it doesn't mean a damn thing."

There were, Kubiak recalls, no further questions for the witness.

———— ★ ————

One of the great things about the Legislature as a lawmaking body is that it deals with the entire range of concerns affecting human life, from education to welfare to sports to civil rights. Unfortunately, often it does not deal with them particularly well. The issues arise, nonetheless, and almost every legislative action provokes an equal and opposite reaction. Bob Leach, a cockfighting advocate from Tyler, had this fulmination against the alleged overregulation by the Legislature: "If God Almighty Hisself wanted to try to create Earth today, he couldn't get a permit to do it."

———— ★ ————

Historically, gun control has been an inviolable taboo for Texas lawmakers. Even assault weapons have a lobby. During the last session, one Austin gun dealer rapturously sang the praises of machine-gun therapy: "They are great to loosen you up. If you work all week, firing one makes you feel more relaxed than a six-pack of beer." (Of course, if you drink and shoot at the same time — whew boy, that'll really mellow you right down!)

Molly Ivins once gave her "weirdest member" award to former Representative Mike Martin of Longview, who paid his cousin to shoot him in the arm with a shotgun, and then claimed he was the victim of a satanic and Communistic cult retaliating against his pro-family and pro-American positions. The cult, he said, was the Guardian Angels of the Underworld. When the law uncovered his scheme, he hid out at his mother's house, where he was found hiding in a stereo cabinet, prompting Molly to pun, "He always did want to be the speaker."

Texas sports are another cherished tradition, as evidenced by the bombardment that Governor Mark White received for his no pass/no play program. At one point, the Legislature even defeated a proposed law that would create a stair-step system of penalties for illegal payments to college athletes, which Senator Carl Parker had characterized: "We are not criminalizing the buying of football players. We're just regulating the price." On the other hand, too often the legislature has given short shrift to educational needs, prompting former Texas Education Commissioner W. N. Kirby to ask: "What better place to start in our fight against ignorance than right here in Austin when the Legislature is in session?"

———— ★ ————

Senator Parker put the matter in proper perspective with this zinger against the opponents of a school-finance reform bill: "Everybody is looking at the price-tag of this bill. What we really need is a fiscal impact statement on the cost of ignorance."

———— ★ ————

Like most Texas senators, Parker received more than his fair share of criticism when the Legislature finally passed the Education Reform Act. This is his account of a typical confrontation, with a typically Parkeresque rejoinder:

> After the Education Reform Act was passed in Texas, imposing the horrible burden of literacy on our public school teachers, many were provoked to the point of real anger directed at those of us who had participated in this terrible crime against humanity.
>
> During the first regular session after enactment of the reform package, a delegation of public school teachers from Houston descended on the office of the Senate Chairman of Education (namely, myself). The leader of the group looked as if she was still mad from having been cut from the traveling squad of the Houston Oilers in spring tryouts. Finding nothing good about the reform package in general, she was particularly irate over the testing provisions requiring teachers to demonstrate literacy, which she chose to characterize as a "competency test."
>
> While I tried mightily to justify the reform package containing parts that I liked and parts that I didn't, she would not be placated, and

finally in utter frustration, turning red in the face, she said to me, "What we really need is for you blamed politicians to take a competency test," to which I replied, "Lady, we couldn't do that, it wouldn't be constitutional."

"Why?" she demanded. "Well," I said, "if we get all the ignorance out of the Texas Legislature, it would no longer be representative government." She didn't think that was very funny.

Molly Ivins used deep East Texas lingo to describe the widespread public view of education reformer H. Ross Perot: "H. Ross went seven bubbles off plumb, crazy as a peach-orchard boar, and announced the trouble with the schools is too much football. That's when we all realized H. Ross Perot is secretly an agent of the Kremlin; yes, a commie, out to destroy the foundation of the entire Texan way of life."

Sometimes Texas schools are named for state leaders. In 1989, when the Legislature voted to expand Central Texas College in Killeen into a four-year institution, thanks largely to the efforts of Representative Stan Schlueter. When the renaming of the school came up for consideration, someone suggested the name of Schlueter Higher Institute of Technology, which prompted one wag to imagine the pep rally that would result when the cheer leaders would call out: "Gimme an S..." and so on.

In the Texas Legislature, human rights issues often provoke a strong reaction, usually negative. For example,

Representative Larry Vick of Houston made these
remarks to an antifeminist group: "The women's rights
movement is the most vicious, conniving, deceiving movement this country has ever seen next to communism."

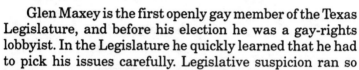

Glen Maxey is the first openly gay member of the Texas
Legislature, and before his election he was a gay-rights
lobbyist. In the Legislature he quickly learned that he had
to pick his issues carefully. Legislative suspicion ran so
high that he had to make this disclaimer about one bill,
"Requiring wheelchair ramps to hotels does not grant civil
rights to homosexuals."

On the other hand, Senator Carl Parker defended a bill
that would require school boards to allow teacher organ-
izations to speak on school policy with this reverse
constitutional argument: "It's sort of a mandatory First
Amendment bill."

Every ten years, all hell breaks loose in the Legislature
in the form of redistricting. Typically, life-or-death strug-
gles develop, with normally friendly, neighborly legislators
desperately attempting to destroy each other in order to
save their own political hides. Redistricting, of course,
produces gerrymandering, the drawing of artistically creative, visually bizarre districts of twisted lines and mythical
shapes. The age-old precept takes hold: "In politics, a
straight line is the shortest distance to disaster."
Hypothetical solutions abound, computer-generated maps
proliferate, and often the whole process ends up mired in
complex, highly politicized court challenges. The process
is downright messy. Jim Harrington, Legal Director of the

Texas Civil Rights Project, made this comment at the conclusion of the last legislative effort, when the House and Senate redistricting bills became law without signature: "Whether you wink at them or kiss them doesn't make the pigs any less dirty."

Senator Carl Parker remarked on the importance for sanity of ignoring the "iffiness" inherent in this legislative process: "If my aunt had been of a different gender, she would have been my uncle."

The legislative process is marked by seemingly endless procedural wranglings. Viewing the reign of chaos on the House floor one day, Representative Eddie Cavazos of Corpus Christi commented: "Do you realize that millions of Chinese are demonstrating for the right to carry on government the way we do?" Given the choice, lawmakers in Austin sometimes seem to prefer political in-fighting and mutual assured destruction over legislating or peacemaking. Welfare Board Chairman Rob Mosbacher noted the popularity of political fisticuffs: "Cooperation has been explained to me in Austin as an unnatural act between non-consenting adults."

Agencies fight agencies, and interest groups fight interest groups, and agencies and interest groups fight each other. Sierra Club leader Ken Kramer reached this conclusion on a Highway Department Sunset bill: "Asking the Highway Department to accept changes to their policy to better protect the environment is like pulling teeth from a dinosaur."

———— ★ ————

Battles continue, nerves fray, trainloads of lobby money pour into the Capitol, but finally the session ends. The time comes for observers to evaluate the final result. Representative Ken Armbrister of Victoria described how he felt at the end of one session: "This whole session has been like chasing a beautiful woman, catching her and turning her around — only to find that she has herpes." Representative Keith Oakley described how the initial attractiveness of the job could kind of wear off: "Being in the Legislature is like having a pet tiger. It's neat to show your friends, but you never know when it'll bite your hand."

———— ★ ————

Sometimes the Regular Session ends and a Special Session begins immediately, then that ends, then another starts, and on and on. Commenting in the middle of the multiple sessions on the worker's comp issue a few years ago, Representative Jim Parker said, "I sat there during the first special session, fat, dumb and happy. I'm still fat, but I'm not as dumb and I'm not at all happy." Looking back on the end of his first session, Senator Bill Ratliff quoted a Biblical line: "The scripture says that the lion and lamb shall lie down together. What the scripture doesn't tell you is that the lamb doesn't get much sleep." (Ambrose Bierce put the same line in wagering terms: "There may come a time when the lion and the lamb will lie down together, but I am still betting on the lion.")

———— ★ ————

With the rush to end the session, many legislators end up voting on bills without even reading them. This led to former Senator Kent Caperton's request just prior to a vote on legislation: "I don't want to start any kind of precedent, but I do want to read your bill for a couple of minutes."

———— ★ ————

The ultimate demonstration of unread legislation started as a joke by then Representative Tom Moore. He introduced a resolution to honor the infamous Boston Strangler, figuring that someone would read the thing before it passed. No one did. The Legislature well earned its own embarrassment after passing the resolution, which provided:

RESOLUTION

WHEREAS, The Honorable Albert De Salvo has unselfishly served his country, his state, and his community; and

WHEREAS, His sincerity, diligence, and cooperation have earned him the warm admiration and affection of his fellow practitioners; and

WHEREAS, Widely esteemed for his knowledge and unique skill, his outstanding service to the public has won him recognition as a model of active citizenship, a champion of worthwhile causes, and an acknowledged leader in his singular field; and

WHEREAS, He has been officially recognized by the State of Massachusetts for his noted activities and unconventional techniques involving population control and applied psychology; and

WHEREAS, Albert De Salvo's singular achievements have brought about significant contributions to the fields of medicine and mental health; and

WHEREAS, Above all, this compassionate gentleman's dedication and devotion to his work has enabled the weak and lonely, throughout our nation, to achieve and maintain a new degree of concern for their future; now therefore, be it

RESOLVED, That the House of Representatives of the 62nd Legislature of the State of Texas commend Albert De Salvo on his outstanding career of public service; and be it further

RESOLVED, That a copy of this Resolution, under the seal of the House of Representatives, be prepared for Albert De Salvo as a token of the continued good wishes of the Texas House of Representatives.

———— ★ ————

With tongue slightly in cheek, State Comptroller Bob Bullock, who served in the House from 1957 to 1959, described the thoughtful process by which he came to vote Yea or Nay on many a bill. "I'd be settin' there in the mornin', hung over as hell, probably been to some lobby party the night before, and a friend would stop by my desk and ask, 'Yuh heard about ol' Joe's bill?'

"I never wanted to let on that I knew no more about ol' Joe's bill than I do about quantum physics, so I'd nod, lookin' as wise as a treeful of owls, and he'd say, 'Bad bill, bad bill.' And I'd nod some more.

"Two minutes later, some freshman'd come by and ask me what I thought of ol' Joe's bill. I'd say, 'Bad bill. Bad bill.' And the two of us would vote against it without ever knowin' what was in it. It was done that way, y'see. It's all done on friendship."

———— ★ ————

During a special session in May, 1982, Baptist preacher Gerald Mann — a Senate chaplain known for his one-line upbeat prayers — intoned to the hushed chamber on opening day: "Lord, may this special session adjourn at least 10 minutes before the devil knows it's convened." Parker couldn't resist an audible: "He already knows. He's the one who called it!"

Political consultant Monte Williams described the general reaction of observers as the usual end of the session rush ensued: "Everybody felt like they were watching their newborn go in for a tattoo." Along the same lines was Representative John Smithee's year-end observation: "What a rowing team and the 70th Legislature have in common is that they both cross the finish line going backwards."

Perennial zealot and government opponent Reverend W. N. Otwell of Fort Worth had this self-righteous shot after the Legislature failed to adopt a budget on time: "The entire Legislature ought to repent." Speaker Gib Lewis offered his own plea, but not to Otwell, at the end of another session: "Well, I just pray that this Session's not remembered at all."

Sometimes they legislate best who legislate least, as recognized by Representative John Cook of Breckenridge in assessing his accomplishments after his first session: "I did not hurt the citizens of the state at all by passing any legislation." Senator Carl Parker gave this evaluation to Representative Gonzalo Barrientos when the latter moved from the House to the Senate: "After you have been in the

House for 10 years, you ain't fit to be anything other than a senator." Other friendly advice Senator Barrientos received at the time: "Barrientos, the main difference between the House and the Senate is that over here we don't gut a member unless we have to!"

Finally, we close this chapter with more Gibberish. At the end of 1991, Speaker Lewis announced that he would not run for another term. Regardless of some of the public controversies that have revolved around Lewis in the press, his popularity with the bulk of the members remained extremely high for an unprecedented period. Moreover, his successor will be hard-pressed to exceed the humor and chuckles that Gib produced through his special command of the language.

> On the tightness of the budget: "We think we have pretty much drained the turnip dry. There's no blood left."
>
> On the state's fiscal outlook: "We're going to do what we have to do with what we have, and I believe we will do that."
>
> On his reelection as Speaker: "I am filled with humidity."
>
> On the need to get on with the state's business: "We need to move along and disperse with objections."
>
> On the negative results of proposed legislation: "It could have bad ramifistations in the hilterlands."
>
> On a developing crisis: "This problem is a two-headed sword: it could grow like a mushing room."

On the desirability of avoiding unnecessary employee terminations while reducing the state work force: "We should not fire people, but accomplish it through employee nutrition."

All legislators have an occasional verbal misstep — such as the time Representative Lloyd Criss called for a "work-free drug place," or when Representative Joe Salem argued that all state revenues should be put into the state treasury because "It just makes good sense to put all your eggs in one basket" — but Gib was the master. Texas should retire the trophy in his honor.

CHAPTER FIVE

Yeller Dawgs and Repubs

By legend, a "yeller dawg" Democrat is someone who would rather vote for a yellow dog than vote for a Republican. At a local officeholder level, Texas remains predominantly Democratic; at last count, 4,607 Democrats occupied state and county offices, versus only 166 Republicans. In years past the numbers were even more lopsided, and John Henry Faulk recalled the time in Texas politics when "Republicans were in such short supply there was talk about establishing a reservation for them."

Railroad Commissioner Lena Guerrero is one of the best at telling this classic yeller dawg story.

> Long ago, in Austin, a skeptical newspaper reporter watching a Democratic parade on Congress Avenue pulled aside one of the marchers and asked him why he was a Democrat. The man replied that his great-granddaddy was a Democrat, his granddaddy was a Democrat, his daddy was a Democrat, and he himself had been a Democrat all his life, whereupon the interrogator asked, "Well, then, if your great-granddaddy, and your granddaddy and your daddy had all been bank robbers, what would you be?" Instantly, the man answered, "I'd be a Republican."

---------- ★ ----------

Lyndon Johnson enjoyed touting the "advantages" of a Republican heart with this story.

"Democrats are the Party with a heart. Not long ago in Houston there was a fellow who was on death's door and rushed down to see one of the Houston transplant doctors. The doctor said, 'Well, you are in luck. We have three hearts in perfect condition that you can choose from. One belonged to a 25-year-old ski champion who was killed in an avalanche. One belonged to a 20-year-old Hollywood dancer who was killed in an automobile accident. And the other belonged to a mean, spiteful, tightfisted 78-year-old Republican banker who died on the operating table just a few minutes ago. Now you can take your choice.'

"Well, without a moment's hesitation the man chose the banker's heart. The operation was successful and the doctor sent the man home and said that he believed he could live a normal life. But just before the man left the doctor said, 'Tell me one thing I don't understand. When you had the choice of an active, healthy, young person's heart, why did you choose that mean old Republican banker's heart?' The man replied 'Because I wanted to be sure that I was getting a heart that had never been used.'"

———————— ★ ————————

Cecil Darby, Jr. relates a similar exchange involving Drury Hathaway, a longtime Runnels County Attorney and Democratic Chairman who had always voted Democratic "no matter who or what was on the ballot." The only group that rivaled the Democratic Party for his devotion was the First Baptist Church of Ballinger. One of Drury's fellow deacons and a Republican asked Drury, "What would you do if Jesus Christ Himself was to run for Governor on the Republican ticket?" Drury paused, thought for a moment, and then said, "I just wouldn't vote."

———————— ★ ————————

Lobbyist Robert Floyd reminisced about growing up in Brady, Texas, and the sound political upbringing that parents then provided their children.

"I remember very clearly my dad's advice about marriage. One day he said to me 'Son, there are two things you must not do when you marry.'"

"'What are those, Dad?' I asked.

"'First, you must not marry a Republican. Second, you must not marry a Catholic.' Later on he did tell me he would forgive me if I married a Catholic!"

Senator Carl Parker once took note of the seriousness of a charge of Republicanism. After successfully fighting off a variety of politically-inspired legal attacks, Parker proudly proclaimed, "I've been accused of everything except liking little boys and voting Republican."

Steve Spurgin, self-professed country lawyer and fourth generation Democrat of Fort Stockton, has warm Democratic memories of his own grandfather, Will Spurgin of Noodle, Texas.

"He was a Democrat, Texan, Presbyterian, and farmer, in that order. Although I was quite mischievous as a youngster, he only took me to the woodshed twice: once when I shot the pet sow with my new Christmas BB gun — and the other time when I called my youngest sister a Republican.

"One of my earliest political memories was the extensive argument my father and grandfather had concerning the Kennedy-Nixon presidential race. The debate began to get quite heated when my father, insufficiently sensitive to the evils of the Republican Party, stated with fervor, 'Nixon is simply the better man!'

"To which my wise grandfather, slamming his fist on the table, replied, 'If he was the better man, he wouldn't be a Republican!'"

———— ★ ————

While the landslide Eisenhower victory in 1952 proved Adlai Stevenson clearly wasn't the choice of the majority of American voters, few candidates have had followers who were more avidly devoted than Adlai's. To illustrate this, there's an election night story that Ernest Joiner, editor of the Ralls, Texas, weekly, told in his paper's first post-election edition in 1952. A rabid pro-Stevenson Democrat, he was downtown listening to returns, and less than an hour after the polls closed, he telephoned his wife.

"Honey," he said, "start packing. Sure as sin, Eisenhower is going to carry Texas, and by golly, I'm ready to move to another state."

A fairly short time later, he called her back, "My dear, you can stop packing. It looks like there won't be any place for us to go."

———— ★ ————

Many years ago when Republicans were few and far between on the Texas political landscape, there was a little rural community where, during presidential elections, invariably there'd be one vote cast for the Republican candidate. No one had ever admitted to being this one maverick, and the locals speculated at length regarding just who the traitor might be. Finally, a consensus developed that it was the wealthy little old gnomelike recluse who lived in a large mansion on a hill. Finally, the old gentleman passed away, so the local pundits felt sure that a Democratic sweep was in the offing. Came the next presidential election, however, and the votes were being counted, when suddenly one of the workers gasped and exclaimed as he held up a ballot, "A Republican vote! My God, we buried the wrong man!"

———— ★ ————

Texas Railroad Commissioner Lena Guerrero began her speech to the 1992 Filing Day Dinner of the Travis County Democratic Party this way. "A man died and went to hell. Miraculously, he then went to heaven. Even more miraculously, after that he came back to life. Everyone was amazed, of course, and a friend asked: 'How do you compare heaven and hell, and which is really better?'

"His answer: 'Well, if you like pearly gates, beautiful white palaces, and streets paved with gold — Heaven is the place. On the other hand, if you want to see your old friends, your favorite relatives, and if you enjoy the warmth of good companionship, then hell's the place for you.'

"Folks, by that definition a Democratic Party Fundraiser is just like hell, and I sure enjoy it!"

———— ★ ————

Democrats sometimes seem to specialize in internecine warfare. Mo Udall has a great description of this underlying organizational dynamic: "When Democrats form a firing squad, they usually arrange themselves in a circle." That fact, in turn, led to Will Roger's classic description of party membership: "I am not a member of any organized political party. I am a Democrat." At a party roast, Ann Richards borrowed from Woody Allen on the Democratic Party's future. "Mankind faces a cross-roads: One Path leads to despair and utter hopelessness. The other path leads to extinction. Let us pray we choose the right path."

———— ★ ————

Deprecation and truth appear pretty much synonymous in Democratic gibes against Republicans. In talking about the Repubs, Will Rogers set a good keynote in reporting on the 1928 Republican convention. "The convention opened with a prayer," he noted. "If the Lord can see his way clear to bless the Republican Party the way it's been carrying on, then the rest of us ought to get it without even asking." Forty years later Harry Truman had a slightly different formulation, one that Lloyd Bentsen still quotes frequently: "I don't give 'em [Republicans] hell; I just tell the truth and they think it's hell." A few more years passed and Adlai Stevenson proposed a cease-fire in these terms: "If the Republicans will stop telling lies about Democrats, we'll stop telling the truth about them."

――――― ★ ―――――

U.S. Representative Bob Eckhardt pointed out the stinginess of Republicans who voted against funds targeted for indigent children: "I'm not so much concerned with the natural bastards as I am with the self-made ones." Similarly, former Senator Ray Farabee of Wichita Falls captured a critical contrast in the parties' respective outlooks. "I am an optimist. If I ever quit being an optimist, I guess I'll become a Republican."

――――― ★ ―――――

To put it simply, Republicans too often protect the rich at the expense of everyone else, and when they're not protecting the rich, they're likely to be pursuing riches. As Mississippi Senator Anselm McLaurin said, "The basic principle that will ultimately get the Republican party together is the cohesive power of public plunder."

――――― ★ ―――――

Former State Representative Charles Gandy tells a story about a young fellow who was hitchhiking on a country road. A car stopped, but before letting him in the car, the driver asked, "Are you a Republican or a Democrat?" "Democrat," said the young man, and the car sped off.

Another car stopped, and the same scenario occurred. This happened several more times, and our hero finally got the message. The next car that stopped was a convertible driven by a beautiful blonde, and she, too, asked, "First, tell me, are you a Republican or a Democrat?"

"Republican," he replied, and sure enough, she let him in.

As they drove along, the wind from the open top began to push the blonde's skirt higher and higher up her legs. The young man found himself getting aroused. Finally, he could control himself no longer and cried out, "Stop. Let me out. My God, I've only been a Republican for ten minutes, and already I feel like screwing somebody!"

True blue Democrats generally question the intelligence of the opposition party. Jim Hightower's observation is standard fare: "Republicans are so empty-headed, they wouldn't make good landfill." Hightower also had two great shots at Republican farm policies.

"You can still make a small fortune in Texas agriculture. Of course, you've got to start with a large fortune."

"What's the difference between a pigeon and an Iowa farmer? The pigeon can still make a deposit on a new tractor."

Molly Ivins expressed well the unavoidable conclusion that, through Reagan, the Republicans demonstrated that "ignorance is no handicap to the presidency."

———— ★ ————

Ever charitable, Democrats attack Republicans' honesty as well as their intelligence. Ann Richards' campaign manager Glenn Smith posited this Republican solution to the state's budget crisis: "If lies were taxable and [Republican] Kent Hance were governor, we could have a huge budget surplus."

———— ★ ————

Extremism in the defense of Republican causes can be some serious extremism. Campaigning in Texas, Michael Dukakis said, "After eight years of massive deficits and the piling up of more debt than all of the presidents from George Washington to Jimmy Carter combined, how can these people call themselves conservatives? They're deficit radicals." Former Senator Hugh Parmer remarked that Repubs appear to moderate only in dire circumstances: "Republicans seem to be against abortion except when the life of their candidates is in danger." By the way, Ann Richards had this shorthand analysis of a particularly illogical (Republican) U.S. Supreme Court decision on abortion: "A young woman may seek permission from a judge and if the judge finds the young woman mature, she may have an abortion. If the court finds her to be immature, she must become a mother."

———— ★ ————

Molly Ivins told of Republican Representative Tom Loeffler, who thought "you get AIDS through your feet" and was "only slightly smarter than a box of rocks." (Newspapers had reported that Loeffler had tied shower caps on his feet before entering the shower stall on a trip to San Francisco!) The closest Loeffler's campaign rhetoric came to profundity was this inanity: "As I have traveled around this state, many people have said to me, 'Texas will never be Texas again.' But I say they are wrong. I say Texas will *always* be Texas."

——————— ★ ———————

Nearly as insightful as Loeffler's statement was Republican gubernatorial candidate Paul Eggers' promise: "I plan to stand up and be counted. And the thing I'm gonna do is, I'm gonna do what we're gonna do right now. I'm going to the people and say, 'Now this is what I'm trying to do.' And I'm going to do this because I believe the people need representation."

——————— ★ ———————

Two-term Republican Governor Bill Clements was a favorite Democratic target. Molly Ivins summed up his political philosophy like this: "If you don't' have an oil well, git one." Garry Mauro explained that Clements was "a self-made man before the days of quality control." Texas Supreme Court Justice Oscar Mauzy, author of the Supreme Court's school-finance decision, said of Clements' delay of court-ordered reform legislation, "I would hope that the governor would either re-read the opinion or have someone read it to him."

——————— ★ ———————

Clements' rhetoric could be his own worst enemy. When a Clements-founded oil company created a huge oil spill that threatened the Texas coast, coldhearted Bill advised the citizenry, "Pray for a hurricane." When he disagreed with a Mexican scholar on immigration, Clements said, "He's just another Meskin with an opinion." He advised the unemployed "to quit settin' around suckin' their thumbs." When Clements began studying Spanish, Agriculture Commissioner Jim Hightower quipped, "Oh, good. Now he'll be bi-ignorant."

———— ★ ————

While a member of SMU's Board of Governors, Clements had approved payments to SMU football players. Later, he evaded the question of whether he told the NCAA the truth about that pay-for-play scandal by answering: "Well, we weren't operating, like on inaugural day, with a Bible."

———— ★ ————

Clements made little effort to placate or work with Democratic legislators. He described Democratic senators as "mating-ritual, wing-thumping" prairie chickens. Questioned by the press on whether that type of comment was helpful to maintain a desirable level of political dialogue, Clements replied: "Well, you know, they have been called worse than that." Jim Hightower retorted: "[Bill Clements] calling you 'bad' is kind of like a frog calling you 'ugly.'"

———— ★ ————

Bob Bullock figured Clements himself could be the solution to budget problems: "We just put a sales tax on BS and make it retroactive to the day Clements started his first term." Bullock explained the anti-vision underlying Clements' approach to budget-cutting, including his punitive elimination of a particular state airplane: "I'm not surprised. If the state had a boat he'd sell that, too. He thinks the world is flat."

———— ★ ————

Clayton Williams was the would-be successor to Clements' title of self-made, self-designated Texas "bidness" hero. What Clayton Williams proved himself to be during the 1990 Texas gubernatorial campaign was the all-time gaffe-master. With the appealing image of a West Texas cowboy made-good, he managed to spend $20 million on the campaign, with some of the best TV commercials in the state's history, yet somehow squander a 30-point lead in the polls and demolish his own election chances. If his handlers could have shot the ads and then shipped Claytie out of state for the duration of the campaign, he might well be governor today.

Author's collection

During one of his campaigns, Bill Clements used billboards in Spanish which opened the door for some fun. The top sign translates as: "Clements, a man of his word." The bottom sign translates as: "Yeah, and my grandmother plays for the Dallas Cowboys."

───────── ★ ─────────

Apparently not satisfied with the temperature of the boiling political hot water he had cooked up for himself, Williams next tried to explain away a rumor about prostitute "honey hunts" on his ranch by claiming that his only experience with prostitutes was when he was a student at Texas A&M and had gone to Mexico to "get serviced." That produced another wave of jokes, such as "How many Republicans does it take to screw in a lightbulb?" Answer: "Republicans don't screw in lightbulbs: They screw in Mexico."

───────── ★ ─────────

Still worse, to explain the servicing remark, or perhaps to show that he had mastered completely the art of digging himself still deeper, Williams said "In the world I live in of bulls and cattlemen, you talk about the bull servicing the cow. I was trying to find a nice, polite term for f_____." Naturally, Williams' remarks generated all sorts of protests. UT student Jennifer Bowles of Austin, for example, responded to Clayton Williams' rape-joke remark with this slogan: "About to be castrated? Just sit back and enjoy it, Claytie."

───────── ★ ─────────

In one of the more bizarre episodes of the 1990 gubernatorial campaigns, which were pretty damn bizarre from start to finish, a flamboyant Austin lawyer who was a defendant in a disbarment suit attempted to subpoena both Richards and Williams (as well as Bullock, Teddy Kennedy, Betty Ford, and others) just a few weeks before election day. The lawyer contended that he needed their testimony in connection with his own defense, because Richards and Bullock, as recovering alcoholics, could provide testimony concerning alcoholism that would somehow explain his own conduct or mitigate his punishment. As to Williams, the allegations rocketed even farther out into space, including:

> Clayton . . . may, likewise, be an alcoholic, but if he is, he is successfully hiding it, even, though, his indiscrete [sic] statements about his personal sexual life and Bordellos in West Texas and across the border in Mexico would indicate that he may have been drinking alcohol when he made those braggadocious [sic] statements, or, outrageous statements, as the case may be, he, Mr. Williams, has been forthright in his confessions of his peccadillos but is suspect as to an addiction, other than alcoholism, which may be termed a whoreholic, defined as the person of the male specie addicted to whores, prostitutes, ladies of the night, Boys' Town — run by madams and pimps, preached over by the Reverend Jimmy Swaggart who leadeth his flock away from righteousness [sic] and along the pathways of parsimony [sic] and sin where donations are usually made beforehand, and in cash, before any clothing is actually removed and the parties assume the horizontal. . . . Meantime, Respondent is obtaining a professional opinion from a psychologist that an addiction to whores can cause a cowboy like Clayton Williams to hate women and want to rope'em and tie'em and drag'em through the dirt as he has threatened to do to his opponent in the Governor's race who happens to be a very nice lady.

The judge quashed the subpoenas.

———————— ★ ————————

Early on in the campaign, even gung-ho Williams' supporter Republican Senator Phil Gramm dejectedly conceded, "There are some of us in politics who can only learn by getting hit up-side the head with a 2-by-4. . . . Claytie had that experience twice."

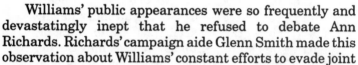

Williams' public appearances were so frequently and devastatingly inept that he refused to debate Ann Richards. Richards' campaign aide Glenn Smith made this observation about Williams' constant efforts to evade joint appearances: "He likes to compare himself with Col. Travis at the Alamo. This is like Col. Clayton Williams drew his famous line in the sand and then told the brave soldiers he was going out for pizza."

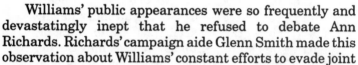

Although chicken to debate Ann, Williams orchestrated and then thoroughly bungled one confrontation with her. He approached Richards at a Dallas forum, after telling a friend (on camera, no less) what he was going to do. He walked up to Ann, who said, "Hello, Claytie," and stuck out her hand to shake his. Williams refused and in a comment seemingly designed to obliterate any remaining shreds of his image as a frontier-type Texas gentleman, said, "I'm not going to shake hands with you. I won't shake hands with a liar."

With grace and dignity, Ann responded, "Well, I'm sorry you feel that way about it, Claytie."

This episode reminded some observers of nothing so much as a Roadrunner cartoon where Wile E. Coyote attempts to shoot the Roadrunner but holds his shotgun backwards and shoots off his own nose.

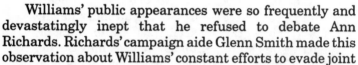

In a final spectacular act of self-immolation on the Friday before Election Day, and after having consistently refused to release his tax returns throughout the campaign, Williams blurted out that "I have paid millions of dollars in taxes. Except in 1986, when I didn't pay anything." The flames lept skyward, voters stampeded towards safety, and Claytie burned to a crisp any lingering possibility of victory.

———— ★ ————

From the Democratic perspective, the Williams' debacle was absolutely delightful. Claytie conclusively proved the accuracy of Ambrose Bierce's counsel: "It's a wise man who profits by his own experience; but it's a good deal wiser man who lets the rattlesnake bite the other fellow." Williams poked his hands into every nook and cranny he could find to try to get rattlesnake bit, and darned if he didn't succeed.

As one wag said, Williams was born silly and apparently has an endless series of relapses.

———— ★ ————

Another observer likened Claytie's consultants to the story of the dog food sales manager. At a sales pep talk, the manager yelled out to his troops, "Who has the best label on their dog food?" The sales force shouted in unison: "We do!"

Then he asked, "Who has the best marketing program?" "We do!" answered the sales force.

"Who has the biggest can?" he shouted. "We do!" they shouted back in unison.

"The best price?" "We do!"

Dropping his voice, and with a glum face, he finished: "Well, then, why aren't we selling any dog food?" The answer, shouted back in vigorous unison: "The dogs won't eat the damn stuff!"

---- ★ ----

Why did anyone support Clayton Williams? Perhaps the best reason came from oilman Eddie Chiles: "He's a good man, he's got a good business mind, he will do a good job, he's my kind of guy, and he's my second cousin."

---- ★ ----

On the presidential level, pseudo-Texan George Herbert Walker Bush has provided Texas Democrats with almost as much grist for the humor mill and about as much fun — except for the part about him getting elected in '88. Few utterances by speakers before national audiences have attracted more attention than Ann's classic quip at the 1988 Democratic National Convention: "Poor George Bush. He can't help it; he was born with a silver foot in his mouth."

---- ★ ----

Jim Hightower also aptly summed up Bush's character: "He's a toothache of a fellow." And in another all-time great put-down of patrician elitism, Hightower said, "His is an upper-class world in which wealth is given to you at birth. George Bush was born on third base and thinks he hit a triple." Hightower also fired this shot at Bush's "stay-the-course" strategy, saying, "If ignorance ever goes to $40 a barrel, I want the drillin' rights on that man's head."

---- ★ ----

Comptroller John Sharp also launched a sharp Sharpism against Bush's disinformation program: "He's treating people the same way that you grow mushrooms — put them in the dark and throw manure on them."

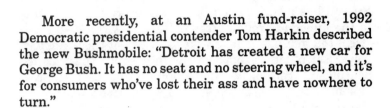

More recently, at an Austin fund-raiser, 1992 Democratic presidential contender Tom Harkin described the new Bushmobile: "Detroit has created a new car for George Bush. It has no seat and no steering wheel, and it's for consumers who've lost their ass and have nowhere to turn."

———— ★ ————

Considerable Democratic dart throwing has targeted Bush's on-again off-again claim of Texas residency. Recently, cartoonist Gary Trudeau encouraged his national readership to send in to Texas Comptroller John Sharp a cartoon form requesting Texas residency, supposedly as a means of avoiding income tax in other states. Thousands of Trudeau readers did so. Even more recently, after the owner of the Houston hotel that Bush claims as his home declared bankruptcy, the *Dallas Morning News* ran a cartoon depicting a Bush-like character sleeping on a bench and covered with newspapers for a blanket, when two obviously homeless types came up and read the headline, which said "Bush's Houston Hotel Files Bankruptcy." One of them asked the other who the sleeper was and the other peeked under the corner of the newspaper blanket and replied simply, "You wouldn't believe me . . . ."

———— ★ ————

On the other hand, Bush also caught well-deserved flack for his 1984 attempt to qualify for a $123,000 tax deduction by claiming his Kennebunkport, Maine, house as his residence.

———— ★ ————

Bush has never shed his aristocratic Ivy League roots — he just doesn't seem Texan. Political satirist Mark Russell has a tune called "Two-gun Georgie Bush," sung to the music of "Yellow Rose of Texas," with these lines: "He'll tell you he's a Texan/though he's got those Eastern ways,/Eatin' lots of barbeque/with a sauce that's called bearnaise." Similarly, Molly Ivins argued that "real Texans" don't use "summer as a verb," don't wear "blue slacks with little green whales all over them," and don't refer to trouble as "deep doo-doo." U.S. Senator John Glenn once asked about "Texan" Bush, "How many Texans do you know whose idea of Mexican food is refried quiche?"

Bush's policies also have attracted enemy fire. Taking note of the fact that the Bush Administration has focused almost exclusively on foreign relations, to the complete exclusion of social and economic issues in these United States, political consultant Hank Morris argued that "Bush thinks a domestic policy is how much he pays his maid." David Axelrod, a media consultant for the Bill Clinton campaign, pointed out that the Administration spends more time on the golf course than on economic policy, and remarked, "When George Bush putts, America goes down the hole."

Ann Richards told this Reagan-Bush yarn in 1988. Ronald Reagan, George Bush, and Jim Wright were on a plane flying over Texas. Reagan took a hundred dollar bill out of his wallet, threw it out the window and said, "I am really going to make someone happy today." George Bush then took 10 ten-dollar bills out of his wallet and threw them out the window, saying "I'm going to make ten people happy today." Jim Wright then asked: "Why don't you both jump out the window and make everyone happy?"

Photo by Y. R. Okamoto. Courtesy of the Lyndon B. Johnson Library, Austin, Texas.

"I always liked small parties, and the Republican party is just about the size I like." Lyndon Johnson.

———————— ★ ————————

Former Land Commissioner Bob Armstrong had this wisecrack about his friend, former Texan Bruce Babbitt, when Bruce was a 1988 presidential aspirant: "Babbitt believes that the Iran-Contra hearings will establish conclusively that there is a link between Ronald Reagan and the Presidency."

———— ★ ————

The Bush-Quayle capacity for misstatement is probably unmatched in American history (though Reagan was a close competitor, of course) and Bush-isms blossomed during the 1988 campaign. On losing the Iowa straw poll, Bush explained that his supporters were "at their daughters' coming-out parties or teeing up the golf course for that crucial last round." That sort of remark did not exactly cement his solidarity with Middle America. Nor did his comment to a bunch of truck drivers in New Hampshire that he'd like to sit down with them to have a "splash of coffee."

———— ★ ————

Describing with pride his intimate relationship — a little too intimate — with President Reagan, he said, "For seven and a half years I have worked alongside [Reagan], and I am proud to be his partner. We have had triumphs, we have made mistakes, we have had sex." He later corrected that to say "setbacks."

———— ★ ————

After a confrontation with Dan Rather, Bush crowed, "It was like combat . . . that guy makes Lesly Stahl look like a [wimp]." Speaking of combat, Bush described for the *Wall Street Journal* his thoughts as his plane went down during World War II. "Well, you go back to your fundamental values. I thought about Mother and Dad and the strength I got from them. And God and faith, and the separation of church and state." Whereupon Molly Ivins asked, "Who among you shall be so churlish as to doubt that our man Bush was contemplating the separation of church and state as his plane hurtled toward the sea?"

———— ★ ————

At another point Bush misdeclared his egalitarianism, by using one too many anti's: "I hope I stand for anti-bigotry, anti-Semitism, anti-racism."

Nor had Bush learned much by 1992. He did little to demonstrate how in-touch he was with average America when he went shopping at a grocery store and expressed slack-jawed amazement that check-out stands were now equipped with electronic scanners to determine prices. Clearly, twenty years of Administration isolation had insulated him from check-out line realities. Bush performed at about the same level with the popular music crowd, when at a fund-raising event he tried to refer to the Nitty Gritty Dirt Band, and what came out was "Nitty Ditty Nitty Gritty Great Bird." Groceries, music, "Sesame Street" — it's all pretty much the same in the White House!

Defending Quayle on the NBC "Today Show" in 1988, Bush started sounding like the VP himself: "My running mate took the lead and was the author of the Job Partnership Training Act. Now, because of a lot of smoke and frenzying of blue fish out there, going after a drop of blood in the water, nobody knows that." It's amazing how much confusion those smoky blue fish can cause!

Is it genetic or environmental with Republicans? Bush understudied with Reagan, Quayle with Bush. Often, they all sound equally confused and out of touch. Whatever the cause, by late 1991 the overwhelming majority of Americans had concluded that Bush should replace Quayle on the Republican ticket. Even among

Republicans, only 39 percent thought Bush should select Quayle again for VP.

———— ★ ————

Quayle jokes are endless. Indeed, an entire publication devoted to that art form, the *Quayle Quarterly*, has flourished. Voter registration activist Lafe Larson offered these representative examples of Quayle humor:

- What were Dan Quayle's toughest three years in school? Second grade.
- What's the difference between chicken, turkey, and Quayle? Nothing.
- Dan Quayle thinks an F-14 is his law school grade. He thinks a B-1 is a multi-vitamin.
- What did Mickey Mouse get for Christmas? A Dan Quayle watch.

———— ★ ————

In the preeminent political insider journal, *Texas Weekly*, Sam Kinch, Jr. reported (with tongue in cheek) this top-secret item on the Bush Administration's plan to bail out the savings and loan industry: it provided for the issuance of Quayle bonds — which have no principal, carry no interest, and never mature.

———— ★ ————

In Quayle's case, the truth is often stranger, and funnier, than any fictional humor could ever be. the *Washington Post*, for example, gave this report of Quayle's "pornographic doll" purchase: "Question: What major political figure who suffers from an image problem would buy a risque, if not obscene, gag doll in full view of hundreds of onlookers — including his horrified wife and a gaggle of reporters?

"Answer: Vice President Dan Quayle.

"Quayle was visiting Chile for the inauguration of President Patricia Aylwin. Shopping for souvenirs, Dan came across the doll. 'I could take this home, Marilyn. This is something teenage boys might find of interest.'

"Over Marilyn's protests, Dan gave a Secret Service agent the money to purchase the doll. Quayle plans to 'pull it out at the appropriate time' at press conferences. Marilyn, with a smile on her face, told him, 'You're so sick.'

"Press Secretary David Beckwith later joked that Quayle had been on a secret buying mission for the National Endowment for the Arts."

Perhaps Quayle's most infamous verbal stumble was his attempt to quote the United Negro College Fund motto, "A mind is a terrible thing to waste," which he garbled into this: "What a waste it is to lose one's mind, or not to have a mind is being very wasteful."

Unfortunately, the Vice President is simply unable to read very well. Interviewed by David Broder and Bob Woodward for a series in the *Washington Post*, several times Quayle mentioned a book he had read, *Modern Times*, which was a critique of collectivism and the welfare state; he even said he had reread parts of it during his last August vacation. In a final interview they asked him what he took away from the book that was "important in the way you look at the world"?

"Well," he explained with the patented Quayle-style lucidity, "I just think that from my strictly historical view of the 20th century, that is probably, that is, you know, the best book I've certainly read. And he goes through it; he starts around the turn of the century up through Vietnam. And it is a very good historical book about history."

Asked the follow-up question of what overall concept he had extracted from the book, Quayle clarified the matter. "Well, I think that the concept, you know — you go through how Hitler, you know, grows to power — sees these types of people that are able to feed on the moment — how he has a huge popular support in Germany at the time. It got into the whole, the arms control aspect, and the decline of the defense posture before World War II.

"He has a very good — and it was something I hadn't thought of, and it's not my area of expertise — and that's how the economic, the international economics, played in all these problems that we had in the 20th century. But there is a rise of these totalitarian leaders. Lenin — a lot of good stuff on Lenin and Stalin."

As Jim Hightower said, "Jay Danforth Quayle, III is a guy whose tongue is heavier than his brain." Only heavy-tonguedness or slow-mindedness could explain this Quayle insight, which he shared with the Phoenix Republican Forum: "If we do not succeed, then we run the risk of failure."

Two final examples of favorite Quayle droppings:

- "Hawaii has always been a very pivotal role in the Pacific. It is part of the United States that is an island that is right here."
- "Looking back, I should have pursued philosophy and history and economics and things of that sort in college more, but I didn't. But I am not going to cry over spilt milk and that's past me."

CHAPTER SIX

Lyndon B. Johnson

Lyndon Johnson's humor was that of a great storyteller in the best old-time Texas tradition. Often his stories were warm, and usually the setting was rural, grounded in his Hill Country origins — parables and yarns told in a rich and rambling style, unmistakably Texan. As one elderly Texas lady exclaimed shortly after Johnson assumed the presidency, "Well, at least we're finally going to have a president without an accent."

Here's a typical LBJ example. "I am reminded of the time when I went to the neighbors' house to ask the lady if her little boy could go home and spend the weekend with me. He was a rather fat little boy. He weighed about 200 and he was about 14 years old. We called him Bones. He was very properly nicknamed Bones. And when I insisted with his mother that she let him go home with me, Bones also asked about his little brother, and finally the mother said no he can't go. His little brother thought that was unjust and he looked up to his mother and he said 'Mama, why can't I go home with Lyndon and spend the night. Bones has done been two-wheres and I haven't been anywheres.'"

---- ★ ----

Another hometown tale that Johnson recited many times, in several variations, was to make a point about public policy "wrecks."

"One of our local boys was inducted into the service. When they were trying to determine his aptitudes and figure out just where he would be assigned, they gave him an IQ test. And they asked him what he would do if he saw a train coming over the hill going 100 miles an hour from north to south, and another one coming from south to north going about 80 miles an hour, and they were two miles apart on the same track. Without hesitating a moment, he said 'I would run and get my brother.' And the induction officer asked 'Well, why would you want to get your brother?'

"'Because he ain't never seen a train wreck.'"

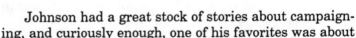

Liz Carpenter tells about the childhood origins of LBJ's preference for doing things impromptu. LBJ once told Liz that "he didn't like to announce his schedule because once when he was a kid in Johnson City, he had taken the day off work to go to New Braunfels to see Vice President Charles Curtis come through." As LBJ told it, "I waited there all day. He never showed up. I was deeply disappointed. I don't want to disappoint people."

"He loved to surprise the press, and he refused to be fenced in by schedules," Liz said, quoting Bonnie Angelo of *Time* magazine, who once said, "When I come to the White House each morning, I don't know whether I'll be spending the day in the West Wing or in West Texas."

On the same point, Bill Moyers told of receiving a phone call one day in his office from the President: "Bill, I'm going to Honolulu."

"Fine, Mr. President, I'll be right over and talk to you about it. Where are you?"

"Over Los Angeles," LBJ replied.

Johnson had a great stock of stories about campaigning, and curiously enough, one of his favorites was about illegal voting. Two fellows were copying names from graveyard tombstones just before a Texas election. One of them came to a tombstone so old and worn that the name was unreadable, but he labored over the stone, squinting and straining to try to read the name. Finally, his partner came over and said, "Come on, leave that one and let's go." "No," said the reader," "This man's got every bit as much right to vote as all the rest of these fellows here."

LBJ's fascination with politics began at a very young age, and he sometimes told a story about a young man who was late for work one day after listening to a political speech. His boss asked why he was late, and the boy explained, "I was listening to a United States Senator make a speech."

The boss said, "Surely the senator didn't speak all this time, did he?" The boy said, "Mighty near, mighty near."

The boss asked, "Well, who was the senator and what did he talk about?"

The boy replied, "Well, his name was Senator Joseph Weldon Bailey from Texas, and I don't recall all that he talked about, but the general impression I got was that he was recommending himself most highly."

LBJ would add, "It is naturally to be assumed that I would recommend myself most highly."

LBJ also liked to tell one of Sam Rayburn's favorite campaign stories, about legendary Texas Congressman Wright Patman. A vacancy developed for a district judge position in a county in Wright Patman's congressional district. The two candidates were speaking before a crowd gathered in the courthouse square. The first candidate had graduated with highest honors from the University of Texas Law School, was selected for law review, and had practiced law for several years in one of the largest, most prestigious law firms in Dallas. Two years before this judicial race, he had run for Congress against Wright Patman and, of course, had been defeated. The second candidate had received his degree from a small night school.

The candidates spoke to the crowd, and the first lawyer talked at length about his education, honors, and experience, and mentioned that his opponent only had a night school permit to practice law and had never gone to the university and didn't have a high level of legal experience; he concluded, "that's too bad, but it's no reason to put him on the bench."

The other poor lawyer then got up to speak and said, "That's true. I didn't get to go to the university and I didn't have those chances. I belonged to a big family. There were nine of us and I had to work to help the girls get through high school. I did have to go to night school to get a permit to practice law. And I haven't worked for any big firm. My legal experience is quite limited. But I do submit one fact for your earnest consideration: I did have the good sense not to run against Wright Patman."

In times of bad news, to put things in perspective Johnson liked to tell a Sam Rayburn story about a letter from a constituent. "He wrote that one of his bald-faced heifers had broken her back and died, that some hunters had set fire to his oatfield stubble, that a tornado had blown down his windmill, that storms had killed all his chickens, that the rain had soaked his oats so they couldn't be stored. And he ended his letter by saying, 'Hope you are the same, I am truly yours. . .'"

A story that Lyndon Johnson enjoyed recounting to emphasize the importance of his goals for America was about Winston Churchill and a visit he received from a delegation of ladies of the Temperance Union during the traumatic days of World War II.

"Mr. Prime Minister," the leader began sternly, "we have been advised that if all the alcohol and brandy you have consumed during this war were emptied into this room, the liquid would come up to about here." She pointed to a spot higher than her head on the wall of this very large room.

Mr. Churchill grimly looked at the spot and said, "My dear lady, so little have I done." He paused, then glancing upward at the ceiling and around the room, he sighed, "So much I have yet to do."

On the subject of listening, Johnson liked to give this advice much more than he liked to follow it: "You ain't learning nothing when you're talking."

Johnson had a keen appreciation of, and fascination with, presidential power, and one of the most frequently told anecdotes of his performance as commander-in-chief concerned a time when he was about to board a helicopter. Several helicopters were on the airfield as he approached. He started walking toward one of them, and a young military aide ran up to him to point out another. "Sir, your helicopter is over there," the young man directed.

LBJ turned to the fellow and said in his slow deep drawl "Son, they're all my helicopters."

Johnson had a fondness for electronic gadgetry. When he was Majority Leader of the U.S. Senate, the limousine assigned to him had a mobile telephone, a perk not given

Minority Leader Everett Dirksen at the time. For a while, Dirksen was jealous about this disparity, but finally he finagled a mobile phone for his own vehicle. He could hardly wait until both he and Johnson were in their respective cars at the same time so that he could call Lyndon and impress him with his newly acquired technological status. When aides alerted him one day that Johnson was in his car, Dirksen immediately went to his car, and placed a call to LBJ's car. When Lyndon answered, Dirksen said, "Hello, Lyndon, this is Ev. I'm calling from my limousine." There was a brief pause, then Lyndon answered, "Fine, Ev. Say, do you mind holding for a minute? My other phone is ringing."

John Kennedy had two stories illustrating LBJ's not inconsiderable ego. The first dealt with the 1960 battle for the Democratic nomination, involving Kennedy, Stu Symington, and Johnson. As Kennedy told it:

"Several nights ago, I dreamed that the good Lord touched me on the shoulder and said, 'Don't worry, you'll be the Democratic Presidential nominee in 1960. What's more, you'll be elected.' I told Stu Symington about my dream. 'Funny thing,' said Stu, 'I had exactly the same dream about myself.'

"We both told our dreams to Lyndon Johnson, and Johnson said, 'That's funny. For the life of me, I can't remember tapping either of you two boys for the job.'"

Kennedy also recalled that on election night in 1960 Johnson called in to report some election results on the Kennedy-Johnson ticket: "Lyndon says WE are winning in Texas but I am losing in Ohio."

As President, LBJ became increasingly conscious of the limits of power. In his 1964 stump speech, LBJ said it was futile for any country to try to rule the world by ultimatum. "A long time ago I learned that telling a man to go to hell and making him go are two different propositions."

Bob Hardesty, a speech writer and confidant of LBJ, tells about a time shortly before LBJ's death when he referred to the pressures of the Presidency during a civil rights seminar at the LBJ Library. LBJ heard President Nixon roundly criticized by various civil rights leaders. When Johnson spoke, he admonished the critics that if they hoped to accomplish anything, they were going to have to reach an accommodation with the President in order to reason with him. Johnson followed with this parable to remind the audience that his advice came from his own experience.

"Out in my little town," he said, "Court Week is very exciting. All the boys leave town to avoid the Grand Jury, and all the citizens go to the court to hear the proceedings. The town drunk, hung over, came up to the hotel one morning as the old judge was leaving and said, 'Would you give a poor man a dime for a cup of coffee?'

"And the judge said, 'Hell, no, get out of the way. I wouldn't give a tramp anything.' The poor fellow with the hangover walked away dejectedly, and just as soon as he got to the end of the porch, the judge said, 'Come back. If you'd like a quarter for a pick-me-up, I'd be glad to help you.' And he handed the old fellow a quarter.

"The drunk looked at him, startled at first, but then with great appreciation in his eyes and said, 'Judge, you've been there, haven't you?'"

When referring to diplomatic negotiations, LBJ sometimes would recall Mark Twain's story of visiting a friend
in New Hampshire. "Mark Twain was walking along the
road and he asked a farmer, he said 'How far is it to
Henderson's place?' 'About a mile and a half,' the farmer
answered. He walked a while longer and he met another
farmer and he asked the same question, 'How far to the
Henderson's place?' And he said 'About a mile and a half.'
And he walked a while longer and he met a third farmer
and he asked again 'How far is it to Henderson's place.' He
said 'About a mile and a half.' Said Twain, 'Thank God I
am holding my own.'"

———————— ★ ————————

LBJ had a good story to illustrate some of the frustrat-
ing costs of government in Washington. "The Postmaster
General told me about getting a letter from a little boy who
had lost his father and whose widowed mother was having
difficulty making ends meet. And he wrote a letter to the
Lord and said 'Dear God, please send mama $100 to help
with the family.' The letter wound up on the Postmaster
General's desk and he was quite touched by it. And he at
that time still had a little money left over from what he
had earned at Prudential. So he took a $20 bill out of his
pocket and put it in a postmaster general's envelope, put
an airmail stamp on it and sent it to the little boy. About
two weeks letter he got a letter back from the boy that said
'Dear God, I'm much obliged for all you've done. It was a
great help. We appreciate it. But we need another $100. If
you don't mind when you send it to mama this time, don't
route it through Washington because they deducted 80%
of it.'"

———————— ★ ————————

"We're all equal around here, but ya'll keep your coats on."

Johnson was a perfectionist, a harsh taskmaster for himself and others, particularly his staff. "There are no favorites in my office," he once said. "I treat them all with the same general inconsideration." He made that point pretty well with this comment about another aide. "He doesn't have sense enough to pour piss out of a boot with the instructions written on the heel."

Another typical Johnson story went back to World War II when John Connally was an aide to then Congressman Lyndon Johnson. This was during the days of rationing, and it seems that Zephyr Wright, the Johnson cook, called Nellie Connally on the telephone. The conversation went something like this:

Zephyr: "Miz Connally, Mr. Johnson is having some very important company Saturday night, and so that we can serve them a fine dinner, he asked me to call and ask can you let us have some of your red stamps for meat."

Nellie: "Now, Zephyr, Mr. Johnson is no more entitled to extra red stamps than anyone."

Zephyr: "Yes, Miz Connally. You know that and I know that, but Mr. Johnson, he don't know that, and I'm not the one that's gonna tell him!"

Bob Hardesty recalled another story that Johnson told, and that his staffers sympathized with, about a boy who had misbehaved and whose papa took him upstairs to administer an old-fashioned spanking. Just as the father was about to strike, the kid asked, "Dad, did your father paddle you?"

Dad: "Yes." "Did his father paddle him?" "Yes." "And did his father paddle him?" "Yes, why?" "Well, don't you think it's about time we put a stop to this inherited brutality?"

Hardesty recalled an additional Johnson story to "make a point" with staff and others. A boyhood friend (now a judge) was offended by something Johnson had said, and LBJ asked him if he remembered "old Otto who was in high school with us" and the judge said he did. "Well," continued LBJ, "Otto got beered up one Saturday night and went to a dance in Stonewall and announced he could 'lick any Dutch son-of-a-bitch in the house.' A German farm boy with biceps the size of boulders grabbed him by the collar and demanded, 'Vot you say?'

"'I said I could lick any Dutch son-of-a-bitch in the house,' Otto repeated. 'Are you a Dutch son-of-a-bitch?'

"'You better not believe it,' said the boy, tightening his grip.

"'Well then,' said Otto, 'I wasn't talking about you.'

"And I wasn't talking about you," the President added. "But the point is still valid."

Once a Senator complained to another when the hard-driving Majority Leader Lyndon Johnson kept the Senate working late. "What's the hurry? Rome wasn't built in a day."

"No," sighed the other Senator, "but Lyndon Johnson wasn't foreman on that job."

Another former United States Senator told a story about Johnson's famous workaholism. About 4:30 a.m. one morning, a ringing phone startled the Senator from his deep slumber. He was even more surprised to hear the President's voice on the phone. "Did I wake you?" the President asked. Whereupon the Senator replied, "Oh, no, Mr. President. I was lying here just hoping you would call."

———— ★ ————

LBJ was a master builder. He constructed and oversaw legislative programs on a scale of greatness achieved by no other president except for FDR. He believed in government, believed in making government work, and believed that creating good legislation was much more difficult — and much more important — than criticizing or destroying legislative initiatives. To drive that point home, he was fond of quoting one of Sam Rayburn's caustic witticisms: "Any jackass can kick over a barn. It takes a carpenter to build one."

———— ★ ————

Hardesty also recounted this story that Johnson would tell on politicians who were always against everything new. "We used to have folks like that around the store in Johnson City. We called them dyspeptics. When the railroad came through town for the first time, one old man stood there and looked at it and said, 'They'll never get the damn thing started.' Then the young lady who was to christen the new train smashed a huge wine bottle across the snout of the locomotive, which immediately took off, soon reaching what was for those times a breakneck speed of 15 or 20 miles an hour. The old codger watched the train leave and commented, 'They'll never get the damn thing stopped.'"

———— ★ ————

Although LBJ was often a moderate liberal on domestic social issues, he was impatient with ideological rigidity, at least where it interfered with getting the job done. One of his Depression-era tales made the point well.

A young man, desperate for a job, appeared before a school board in a small Texas Hill Country community to apply for a teaching position. The would-be teacher did a fine job during the interview. Finally, after conferring with his colleagues, the school board president said, "Young man, we are impressed with you and inclined to give you this job as our teacher. But, we have one more question, a matter of geography about which there is some difference of opinion in our community, and we'd like to know which side you're on. Do you teach that the world is round, or do you teach that it is flat?" The young man responded, "Sir, I can teach it either way."

Johnson's ego, of course, was immense, but he also could poke fun at himself. On a visit to the LBJ ranch, Germany's Ludwig Erhard told Johnson, "I understand you were born in a log cabin, Mr. President." "No, Mr. Chancellor," Johnson replied, "I was born in a manger."

Federal Judge Barefoot Sanders tells the story of a certain congressman who became greatly distressed because, despite his entreaties, he was unable to gain an audience with President Johnson. One day he appeared and literally begged the staff to get him in to see the President. Finally, one of the besieged staffers gave in, and relayed the request to LBJ, "Sir, the Congressman says that it's terribly important that he really does need to see you." LBJ responded, "Okay — send him my picture."

Senator Lloyd Bentsen tells of a quail shoot in South Texas with President Johnson and some other friends. "One of our friends had commissioned a painting of the hunt," Bentsen explained, "so we had an artist along."

"The artist took photographs and used one of those to prepare five identical paintings, with each painting showing LBJ standing behind the dogs and shooting at quail. Behind LBJ, watching him shoot, were John Connally, myself, George Brown and L. F. McCollum.

"Each of us received a painting of the scene and we were duly impressed by the real-life depiction and accuracy captured by the artist — that is, all of us were except for Lyndon. He returned his painting to the artist with instructions that it be repainted so that instead of showing one quail falling it showed two."

At a presidential lunch one day, Bill Moyers was saying grace, when Johnson bellowed: "Speak up, Bill! I can't hear a damn thing." Moyers looked up and said quietly, "I wasn't addressing you, Mr. President."

Johnson recognized his own tendency to exaggerate, and he told a Darrell Royal story to poke fun at himself and other persons similarly afflicted.

Darrell sent one of his all-Americans up to the Washington Redskin team to try to make the team. Otto Graham himself interviewed the player.

Graham said, "Tell me about yourself young man. I know that you made all-American. I know that you are from the University of Texas. And I know that you are a triple threat man. But just give me some specifics."

The youngster said, "Well, Mr. Graham, I can run the 100 yards in 9 seconds on a muddy field and I averaged 25 yards every time I carried the ball."

Graham said, "Well, that's great, son. What about your passing?"

"Well, I was the principal passer on our championship team. We have a lot of wind in football season down our way, and my average pass was 64 yards against the wind last year."

And Graham said, "That's remarkable. What about your punting?"

The boy said, "71 yards, sir, average for the season."

"Well," Graham said, "That's all quite amazing. You know, most of us have our pluses and minuses, our weaknesses as well as our strengths. Tell me of any problems you have."

The boy said, "Coach, I guess I do tend to exaggerate a little."

★

Johnson told another story of pride, this one about national pride. "A prominent Frenchman was talking to an Englishman one time. He said in a rather condescending way, 'I think if I had not been born a Frenchman I think I would have liked to have been born an Englishman.'

"And the Englishman responded and said 'I understand. If I had not been born an Englishman I would have wanted to have been born an Englishman.'

"And I say to you today that I am proud that I was born as American and if I had not been born an American I think as I look this world over, I would have wanted to be born an American."

★

Ever conscious of the need to maintain at least the appearance of humility, Johnson once burst out of the Oval Office with a draft of a crucial speech, shouting to his speech writers, "Now listen, you sons of bitches, this just won't do. I want this rewritten, and I want you to put some stuff in here to make me sound goddamn humble!"

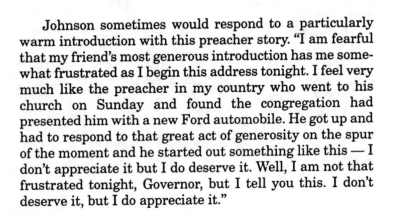

Johnson sometimes would respond to a particularly warm introduction with this preacher story. "I am fearful that my friend's most generous introduction has me somewhat frustrated as I begin this address tonight. I feel very much like the preacher in my country who went to his church on Sunday and found the congregation had presented him with a new Ford automobile. He got up and had to respond to that great act of generosity on the spur of the moment and he started out something like this — I don't appreciate it but I do deserve it. Well, I am not that frustrated tonight, Governor, but I tell you this. I don't deserve it, but I do appreciate it."

Another LBJ preacher story focused on the need for vigilance.

"One Sunday a preacher down in my country saw a member of his congregation fall asleep and start snoring. The preacher held his tongue. The next Sunday, though, the same thing happened. Again the preacher ignored the distraction and said nothing. But the third Sunday, the same thing happened again, and the preacher finally got tired of it and he decided he'd play a little joke on the sleeper.

"And while he was sleeping, the preacher said in a rather low voice 'All of you folks that want to go to heaven, please stand.' And everybody stood except the fellow on the front row that was sleeping and snoring. And when they sat down he said in a very loud voice 'Now all of you folks that want to go to hell, please stand.'

"That stirred the fellow and he woke up and he heard the word 'please stand' so he jumped up. He looked around and saw that no one else was standing with him and he said 'Preacher, I don't know what it is we are voting on but you and I seem to be the only two who agree on the matter."

Another good Johnson anecdote about humility came from the campaign trail. In 1960 when his whistle-stop train was passing through Culpepper, Virginia, he had just finished his speech to his depot audience when the train started pulling down the track. He shouted over the microphone: "Tell me, what has Dick Nixon ever done for Culpepper?" "Hell," an old man shouted back, "what has ANYBODY ever done for Culpepper?"

Along the same lines, LBJ told a story about the New York financial community. He said the story was about Truman, or maybe FDR, both of whom he said were "never real popular with the financial community."

"There was a Wall Street broker who would go by the newsstand every morning and buy a copy of the New York Times. They were selling for a nickel in those days, and he'd put a nickel down to pay for it. He'd pick up the paper, look at page one and then put the paper down and walk away. He did that for several months.

"Finally, one day the vendor said 'Mister why do you come here every morning, buy the paper, pay for it, and then walk off and leave it? Why don't you take it with you?'

"The man replied 'Because young man, I am interested only in the obituaries.'

"'But the obituaries are in the second section of the paper about page 38 or 40 and you never look beyond the front page.'

"'Well,' he said, 'the so-and-so I am interested in is going to be on the front page.'"

──────── ★ ────────

Finally, we sympathize with Johnson's remarks on one of his own books. "I've been working on my own book. It won't be out until next year. It will review the highlights of my administration. While I haven't submitted any of the manuscripts yet, I already have seven unfavorable reviews."

SOURCE NOTES

The items below identify sources that are not obvious in the main text or that are attributable to specific locations in other books or other published sources. References that merely name a particular individual indicate that the authors first heard or obtained the item from the individual named.

Preface

Humor antidote: Morris K. Udall, *Too Funny To Be President* (Henry Holt and Company, Inc. 1988), p. xiv.

Garfield/"solemn as an ass": Morris K. Udall, *Too Funny To Be President*, p. xv.

Coolidge/"solemn as an ass": Morris K. Udall, *Too Funny To Be President*, p. 235.

Shields/copyright: Morris K. Udall, *Too Funny To Be President*, p. 191.

Buchwald/credit: Morris K. Udall, *Too Funny To Be President*, p. 191.

Chapter One. Introduction(s)

Cancer of the sound bite: John Tierney, "Celebrating the Sound Bite," *New York Times*, January 23, 1992, p. A1.

Bonilla story: Steve Bartlett.

Program chairman: Morris K. Udall, *Too Funny To Be President*, p. 241.

Let me off: Morris K. Udall, *Too Funny To Be President*, p. 129.

Treed banker: Sam Kinch, Jr., *Texas Weekly*, February 19, 1988, p. 6.

Sleep like a baby: Sam Kinch, Jr., *Texas Weekly*, October 10, 1988, p. 6.

Perot extinguished: Mark McCulloch.

Chapter Two: The Campaign Trail

Run for sheriff: Morris K. Udall, *Too Funny To Be President*, p. 232.

High expectations: Molly Ivins, *Molly Ivins Can't Say That, Can She?* (Random House, Inc. 1991), p. 276.

Fry-Off: Molly Ivins, *Molly Ivins Can't Say That, Can She?*, p. 277.

Cannibals: Morris K. Udall, *Too Funny To Be President*, p. 31.

Biting voters: Morris K. Udall, *Too Funny To Be President*, p. 224.

Jim Wright: Morris K. Udall, *Too Funny To Be President*, p. 224.

JFK/Alamo: Morris K. Udall, *Too Funny To Be President*, p. 237.

Butterhair: Molly Ivins, *Molly Ivins Can't Say That, Can She?*, p. 100.

Parmer/Gramm: Sam Kinch, Jr., *Texas Weekly*, March 12, 1990, p. 6.

Mattox/lace underwear: Sam Kinch, Jr., *Texas Weekly*, October 9, 1989, p. 6.

Barrera/mudslinging: Molly Ivins, *Molly Ivins Can't Say That, Can She?*, p. 47.

Mattox/treatment: Sam Kinch, Jr., *Texas Weekly*, March 12, 1990, p. 6.

Luce/Hee Haw: Sam Kinch, Jr., *Texas Weekly*, March 12, 1990, p. 6.

Rains/Roy Rogers: Sam Kinch, Jr., *Texas Weekly*, March 19, 1990, p. 6.

Mauro/losing money: Sam Kinch, Jr., *Texas Weekly*, April 15, 1991, p. 6.

Bentsen/possum: Sam Kinch, Jr., *Texas Weekly*, October 17, 1988, p. 6.

Babbit/back: Morris K. Udall, *Too Funny To Be President*, p. 199.

Texas humanism: Molly Ivins, *Molly Ivins Can't Say That, Can She?*, p. 4.

Yuppie toilet seats: Sam Kinch, Jr., *Texas Weekly*, October 14, 1985, p. 6.

Maverick/bastards: Richard Henderson, *Maury Maverick: A Political Biography* (University of Texas Press 1970), p. 303.

Maverick/chigro: Richard Henderson, *Maury Maverick: A Political Biography*, p. 303.

Maverick/death: Richard Henderson, *Maury Maverick: A Political Biography*, p. xvii.

Rabid will maker: Mo Udall tells an almost identical version of this story. Morris K. Udall, *Too Funny To Be President*, p. 207.

Maverick/constituents: Richard Henderson, *Maury Maverick: A Political Biography*, p. 182.

Neutrality hell: Morris K. Udall, *Too Funny To Be President*, p. 209.

Yellow stripes and armadillos: Sam Kinch, Jr., *Texas Weekly*, July 23, 1984, p. 4.

Skunk ribbons: Sam Kinch, Jr., *Texas Weekly*, May 26, 1986, p. 6.

Larger foxes: Sam Kinch, Jr., *Texas Weekly*, October 6, 1986, p. 6.

Rains affording: Sam Kinch, Jr., *Texas Weekly*, October 9, 1989, p. 6.

Garcia/fund-raiser eqiquette: *Austin American Statesman*, August 31, 1990, p. A17.

Perot buys God: "When the State Bar Turns Standup Comic," *Texas Lawyer*, January 29, 1990, p. 20.

Politician piles: Sam Kinch, Jr., *Texas Weekly*, February 25, 1991, p. 6.

Manure baptism: Sam Kinch, Jr., *Texas Weekly*, January 8, 1990, p. 6.

Press chiggers: Sam Kinch, Jr., *Texas Weekly*, June 27, 1988, p. 6.

Overpaid, overprivileged: Richard Henderson, *Maury Maverick: A Political Biography*, p. xx.

Military reading: Richard Henderson, *Maury Maverick: A Political Biography*, p. 102.

Hightower/ads: *Austin American Statesman*, November 8, 1990, p. A19.

LBJ/church: Morris K. Udall, *Too Funny To Be President*, p. 239.

Garcia/journalists' language: *Austin American Statesman*, December 1, 1989, p. A17.

Paper personality: Sam Kinch, Jr., *Texas Weekly*, December 17, 1990, p. 6.

Emancipation Proclamation: Morris K. Udall, *Too Funny To Be President*, p. 234.

Unemployed king: Sam Kinch, Jr., *Texas Weekly*, January 28, 1991, p. 6.

Chapter Three. Politics and Politicians

Maverick/ridiculed: Richard Henderson, *Maury Maverick: A Political Biography*, p. 67.

White weathervane: Molly Ivins, *Molly Ivins Can't Say That, Can She?*, p. 44.

McKinney/artichoke: Sam Kinch, Jr., *Texas Weekly*, December 9, 1985, p. 6.

Bullock/truth-testing: Sam Kinch, Jr., *Texas Weekly*, March 24, 1986, p. 6.

Dirksen/falling: Edward Boykin, *The Wit and Wisdom of Congress* (Funk & Wagnalls Company, Inc. 1961), p. 19.

Politician bullfrog: Bob Murphey.

Wright/Poage lecture: Jim Wright, *You and Your Congressman* (Capricorn Books New York 1976), p. 82.

Churchill coffee: Morris K. Udall, *Too Funny To Be President*, p. 209.

Outliving sumbitches: Morris K. Udall, *Too Funny To Be President*, p. 199.

Bullock/ravage: Sam Kinch, Jr., *Texas Weekly*, February 23, 1987, p. 6.

Bullock/liver: Susan Yerkes.

Barnes/raided: Sam Kinch, Jr., *Texas Weekly*, February 23, 1987, p. 6.

Bullock/ex-wives: Susan Yerkes.

Krier/Parker sleeping together: Susan Yerkes.

Hightower/mixed emotions: Susan Yerkes.

Clements/burns: Susan Yerkes.

Reagan/arrogant: Charles Henning, *The Wit & Wisdom of Politics*, p. 13.

Carr/bravest: Susan Yerkes.

Hightower/pig droppings: Susan Yerkes.

Braided underarms: Susan Yerkes.

Slagle/monotonizes: 1987 Texas Democratic Party Roast of Bob Slagle.

Slagle/knowledge: 1987 Texas Democratic Party Roast of Bob Slagle.

Slagle/thoughts: 1987 Texas Democratic Party Roast of Bob Slagle.

Ann/Mother Teresa: Neal Spelce Austin Letter, January 2, 1988.

Ann/Mrs. Miles: Molly Ivins, *Molly Ivins Can't Say That, Can She?*, p. 76.

Gib/quail: Sam Kinch, Jr., *Texas Weekly*, August 6, 1990, p. 6.

Perry/music BS: Sam Kinch, Jr., *Texas Weekly*, November 5, 1990, p. 6.

Clayton/Boston Strangler: Sam Kinch, Jr., *Texas Weekly*, December 22, 1990, p. 6.

Many ticks: Sam Kinch, Jr., *Texas Weekly*, March 24, 1986, p. 6.

Politics, highway wreck: Sam Kinch, Jr., *Texas Weekly*, December 3, 1990, p. 6.

Politics, football: Sam Attlesey.

Federal judges, friends: "When the State Bar Turns Standup Comic," *Texas Lawyer*, January 29, 1990, p. 20.

Federal judge, god: "When the State Bar Turns Standup Comic," *Texas Lawyer*, January 29, 1990, p. 20.

Federal judge, light bulb: "When the State Bar Turns Standup Comic," *Texas Lawyer*, January 29, 1990, p. 20.

Judges, incest: Franklin Spears, "Selection of Appellate Judges," 40 Baylor L. Rev. 501, 517 (1988).

Speed contests: Burnett, "Observations on the Direct Election Method of Judicial Selection," 44 Tex. L. Rev. 1098, 1099 (1966).

Judges, straight: "When the State Bar Turns Standup Comic," *Texas Lawyer*, January 29, 1990, p. 20.

Judges, good parents: Morris K. Udall, *Too Funny To Be President*, p. 222.

Lawyers, fat targets: "When the State Bar Turns Standup Comic," *Texas Lawyer*, January 29, 1990, p. 20.

Chapter Four. The Lege

Twelve worse: Molly Ivins, *Molly Ivins Can't Say That, Can She?*, p. 8.

Fist fight: Molly Ivins, *Molly Ivins Can't Say That, Can She?*, p. 9.

Clayton/forget: Sam Kinch, Jr., *Texas Weekly*, June 25, 1984, p. 6.

Russell/mouse trap: Sam Kinch, Jr., *Texas Weekly*, March 16, 1987, p. 6.

Hobby/Sesquicentennial: Sam Kinch, Jr., *Texas Weekly*, February 4, 1985, p. 6.

Cavazos/mind meeting: Representative Steve Wolens. A similar item appears in Sam Kinch, Jr., *Texas Weekly*, April 9, 1990, p. 6.

Ottmers/mud-wrestling: Sam Kinch, Jr., *Texas Weekly*, June 11, 1990, p. 6.

Willis/pit bulldogs: Sam Kinch, Jr., *Texas Weekly*, May 27, 1991, p. 6.

Schwartz/seeing-eye dog: Molly Ivins, *Molly Ivins Can't Say That, Can She?*, p. 16.

Brooks/milking alligator: Sam Kinch, Jr., *Texas Weekly*, September 1, 1986, p. 6.

Schlueter picante: Sam Kinch, Jr., *Texas Weekly*, October 6, 1986, p. 6.

Lewis/syntax: Molly Ivins, *The Texas Observer*, February 14, 1992, p. 3.

Richards/soup: Sam Kinch, Jr., *Texas Weekly*, June 18, 1984, p. 6.

Craddick/eat it: Sam Kinch, Jr., *Texas Weekly*, August 3, 1987, p. 6.

Willis/cow: Sam Kinch, Jr., *Texas Weekly*, April 23, 1990, p. 6.

Counts/spittoon drinking: Sam Kinch, Jr., *Texas Weekly*, July 1, 1991, p. 6.

Moncrief/sacred cow: Sam Kinch, Jr., *Texas Weekly*, July 29, 1991, p. 6.

Wells/sacred stampede: Sam Kinch, Jr., *Texas Weekly*, July 1, 1991, p. 6.

Sharp/gimme handful: Sam Kinch, Jr., *Texas Weekly*, July 15, 1991, p. 6.

Hamilton/Moses: Sam Kinch, Jr., *Texas Weekly*, August 12, 1991, p. 6.

Kamel/rob Paul: Sam Kinch, Jr., *Texas Weekly*, September 23, 1991, p. 6.

Sharp/heaven: *The Dallas Morning News*, March 6, 1992, p. 25A.

Hightower/prisons: Sam Kinch, Jr., *Texas Weekly*, July 22, 1991, p. 6.

Stripe city: *Molly Ivins, Molly Ivins Can't Say That, Can She?*, p. 24.

Stiles/one-armed judge: Sam Kinch, Jr., *Texas Weekly*, August 5, 1991, p. 6.

Food stamps: Molly Ivins, *Molly Ivins Can't Say That, Can She?*, p. 11.

Oakley/plaid jacket: Molly Ivins, *Molly Ivins Can't Say That, Can She?*, p. 11.

Lewis/golfings: Sam Kinch, Jr., *Texas Weekly*, July 10, 1989, p. 6.

Smith/Arby's: Sam Kinch, Jr., *Texas Weekly*, September 11, 1989, p. 6.

Smitty/lobby tool: Sam Kinch, Jr., *Texas Weekly*, September 4, 1989, p. 6.

Politicians aren't crooks: Molly Ivins, *Molly Ivins Can't Say That, Can She?*, p. 1, 58.

Lubbock senator: Molly Ivins, *Molly Ivins Can't Say That, Can She?*, p. 64.

Nugent/dracula: Molly Ivins, *Molly Ivins Can't Say That, Can She?*, p. 17.

Feeding hands: Sam Kinch, Jr., *Texas Weekly*, April 8, 1985, p. 6.

Clower/party liberal: Molly Ivins, *Molly Ivins Can't Say That, Can She?*, p. 265.

Johnson/drink smart: Morris K. Udall, *Too Funny To Be President*, p. 247.

Johnson/friends above principles: Jack Johnson, February 15, 1988.

Moore/personal profit: Molly Ivins, *Molly Ivins Can't Say That, Can She?*, p. 59.

Lewis/walnut: Molly Ivins, *Molly Ivins Can't Say That, Can She?*, p. 59.

Wilson/caucus: Molly Ivins, *Molly Ivins Can't Say That, Can She?*, p. 137.

Cryer/raccoon: Sam Kinch, Jr., *Texas Weekly*, March 18, 1991, p. 6.

Sims/thunder: Sam Kinch, Jr., *Texas Weekly*, June 11, 1990, p. 6.

Leach/cockfighting: Sam Kinch, Jr., *Texas Weekly*, May 18, 1987, p. 8.

Machine-gun therapy: Sam Kinch, Jr., *Texas Weekly*, June 3, 1991, p. 6.

Martin/speaker: Molly Ivins, *Molly Ivins Can't Say That, Can She?*, p. 53.

Parker/regulating price: Sam Kinch, Jr., *Texas Weekly*, March 13, 1989, p. 6.

Kirby/legislative ignorance: Sam Attlesey.

Parker/cost of ignorance: Sam Kinch, Jr., *Texas Weekly*, March 26, 1990, p. 6.

Perot/bubbles off plumb: Molly Ivins, *Molly Ivins Can't Say That, Can She?*, p. 24.

Vick/antifeminist: Molly Ivins, *Molly Ivins Can't Say That, Can She?*, p. 13.

Maxey/wheelchair ramps: Sam Kinch, Jr., *Texas Weekly*, May 15, 1989, p. 6.

Parker/First Amendment: Sam Kinch, Jr., *Texas Weekly*, April 3, 1989, p. 6.

Straight line: John P. Roche quoted in Jonathon Green, *The Cynic's Lexicon*, p. 165.

Harrington/pig kissing: Sam Kinch, Jr., *Texas Weekly*, June 24, 1991, p. 6.

Parker/iffiness: Sam Kinch, Jr., *Texas Weekly*, May 15, 1989, p. 6.

Cavazos/Chinese demonstrating: Sam Kinch, Jr., *Texas Weekly*, June 5, 1989, p. 6.

Mosbacher/unnatural act: Sam Kinch, Jr., *Texas Weekly*, April 16, 1990, p. 6.

Kramer/highway dinosaur: Sam Kinch, Jr., *Texas Weekly*, March 25, 1991, p. 6.

Armbrister/herpes: Sam Kinch, Jr., *Texas Weekly*, July 9, 1984, p. 6.

Oakley/pet tiger: Sam Kinch, Jr., *Texas Weekly*, December 18, 1989, p. 6.

Parker/fat, dumb, happy: Sam Kinch, Jr., *Texas Weekly*, December 4, 1989, p. 6.

Ratliff/lamb sleep: Sam Kinch, Jr., *Texas Weekly*, June 19, 1989, p. 6.

Caperton/reads: Sam Kinch, Jr., *Texas Weekly*, March 27, 1989, p. 6.

Bullock/hung over: Molly Ivins, *Molly Ivins Can't Say That, Can She?*, p. 10.

Williams/newborn tattoo: Sam Kinch, Jr., *Texas Weekly*, August 19, 1991, p. 6.

Smithee/rowing backwards: Sam Kinch, Jr., *Texas Weekly*, June 8, 1987, p. 8.

Otwell/repent: Sam Kinch, Jr., *Texas Weekly*, June 29, 1987, p. 6.

Lewis/remembered: Sam Kinch, Jr., *Texas Weekly*, August 19, 1981, p. 6.

Cook/legislate least: Sam Kinch, Jr., *Texas Weekly*, June 10, 1991, p. 6.

Parker/fit to be senator: Sam Kinch, Jr., *Texas Weekly*, July 6, 1984, p. 6.

Lewis/turnip dry: Sam Kinch, Jr., *Texas Weekly*, May 27, 1985, p. 6.

Lewis/what we have: Sam Kinch, Jr., *Texas Weekly*, January 16, 1989, p. 6.

Lewis/humidity: Molly Ivins, *Molly Ivins Can't Say That, Can She?*, p. 61.

Lewis/disperse objections: Molly Ivins, *Molly Ivins Can't Say That, Can She?*, p. 226.

Lewis/hilterland ramifistations: Molly Ivins, *Molly Ivins Can't Say That, Can She?*, p. 226.

Lewis/employee nutrition: Molly Ivins, *Molly Ivins Can't Say That, Can She?*, p. 226.

Criss/work-free drug: Sam Kinch, Jr., *Texas Weekly*, February 20, 1989, p. 6.

Salem/basket: Molly Ivins, *Molly Ivins Can't Say That, Can She?*, p. 14.

Chapter Five. Yeller Dawgs and Repubs

Daddy Democrat: Mo Udall traced a version of this story back to Teddy Roosevelt's 1904 presidential campaign. Morris K. Udall, *Too Funny To Be President*, p. 212.

Hathaway/Jesus: Cecil C. Darby, Jr.

Parker/little boys: Sam Attlesey.

Democratic firing squad: Morris K. Udall, *Too Funny To Be President*, p. 5.

Richards/Woody Allen: Sam Kinch, Jr., *Texas Weekly*, May 29, 1989, p. 6.

Rogers/prayer: Morris K. Udall, *Too Funny To Be President*, p. 5.

Truman/truth: Morris K. Udall, *Too Funny To Be President*, p. 6.

Eckardt/self-made bastards: Morris K. Udall, *Too Funny To Be President*, p. 229.

Farabee/Democratic optimist: Sam Kinch, Jr., *Texas Weekly*, December 9, 1985, p. 6.

Reagan/handicap: Molly Ivins, *Molly Ivins Can't Say That, Can She?*, p. 104.

Smith/Hance lies: Sam Kinch, Jr., *Texas Weekly*, September 4, 1989, p. 6.

Dukakis/deficit radicals: Sam Kinch, Jr., *Texas Weekly*, September 26, 1988, p. 6.

Parmer/Republicans abortion: Sam Kinch, Jr., *Texas Weekly*, April 16, 1990, p. 6.

Richards/Supreme Court: Sam Kinch, Jr., *Texas Weekly*, July 2, 1990, p. 6.

Loeffler/box of rocks, Texas always Texas: Molly Ivins, *Molly Ivins Can't Say That, Can She?*, p. 40.

Eggers/people need representation: Molly Ivins, *Molly Ivins Can't Say That, Can She?*, p. 13.

Clements/oil well: Molly Ivins, *Molly Ivins Can't Say That, Can She?*, p. 45.

Mauzy/Clements to read: Sam Kinch, Jr., *Texas Weekly*, December 11, 1989, p. 6.

Clements/hurricane: Molly Ivins, *Molly Ivins Can't Say That, Can She?*, p. 45.

Clements/bi-ignorant: Molly Ivins, *Molly Ivins Can't Say That, Can She?*, p. 46.

Clements/bible hand: Sam Kinch, Jr., *Texas Weekly*, March 16, 1987, p. 6.

Clements/prairie chickens: Sam Kinch, Jr., *Texas Weekly*, April 6, 1987, p. 6.

Republicans screw in Mexico: Molly Ivins, *Molly Ivins Can't Say That, Can She?*, p. 278.

Williams/bull servicing: Sam Kinch, Jr., *Texas Weekly*,
July 16, 1990, p. 6.

Bowles/Claytie castrated: Sam Kinch, Jr., *Texas Weekly*,
April 2, 1990, p. 6.

Gramm/2-by-4: Sam Kinch, Jr., *Texas Weekly*, June 18,
1990, p. 6.

Smith/Williams pizza: Sam Kinch, Jr., *Texas Weekly*,
May 21, 1990, p. 6.

Williams/self-immolation: Molly Ivins, *Molly Ivins Can't
Say That, Can She?*, p. 282.

Chiles/second cousin: Sam Kinch, Jr., *Texas Weekly*, July
31, 1989, p. 6.

Hightower/Bush third base: Sam Kinch, Jr., *Texas
Weekly*, July 25, 1988, p. 6.

Hightower/drilling rights: Molly Ivins, *Molly Ivins Can't
Say That, Can She?*, p. 116.

Sharp/Bush mushrooms: Sam Kinch, Jr., *Texas Weekly*,
September 26, 1988, p. 6.

Bush/homeless cartoon: *Dallas Morning News*, February
23, 1992, p. 2J.

Russell/Bush bearnaise: quoted in the *New York Times*,
October 7, 1984.

Blue slacks/green whales: Molly Ivins, *Molly Ivins Can't
Say That, Can She?*, p. 113.

Axelrod/Bush putts: John Tierney, "Celebrating the
Sound Bite," *New York Times*, January 23, 1992, p.
A10.

Bush/coming-out parties: Molly Ivins, *Molly Ivins Can't
Say That, Can She?*, p. 118.

Bush/Rather, Stahl: Molly Ivins, *Molly Ivins Can't Say
That, Can She?*, p. 117.

Bush/plane: Molly Ivins, *Molly Ivins Can't Say That,
Can She?*, p. 118.

Bush/anti's: The *New York Times*, January 16, 1992, p.
A14.

Jeffrey L. Yoder, *The Quayle Quarterly* (P.O. Box 8593, Brewster Station, Bridgeport, Ct. 06605).

Quayle bonds: Sam Kinch, Jr., *Texas Weekly*, February 27, 1989, p. 6.

Quayle's pornographic doll: *Washington Post*, March 12, 1990, "The Doll Episode," quoted in *The Quayle Quarterly*, Vol. 1, No. 2, Spring 1990, p. 9.

Quayle/reading: David S. Broder & Bob Woodward, "Waiting in the Wings to Play the Lead Role," *The Washington Post National Weekly Edition*, January 27-February 2, 1992, pp. 8-9.

Quayle/Hawaii: Lucia Schneck, "The Education Vice President," in *The Quayle Quarterly*, Vol. 1, No. 2, Spring 1990, p. 1.

Quayle/past spilt milk: Lucia Schneck, "The Education Vice President," in *The Quayle Quarterly*, Vol. 1, No. 2, Spring 1990, p. 15.

NAME INDEX

ABOUT THE AUTHORS

Charles Herring, Jr. served two terms as Chair of the Travis County Democratic Party (1986-1990) and is a practicing attorney in the Austin office of the law firm of Jones, Day, Reavis & Pogue. He is a lifelong Democrat and began his campaign life handing out pushcards for his father, who served in the Texas Senate from 1956 to 1972. Chuck is the author of many boring articles on legal topics, as well as a new book *Texas Legal Malpractice & Lawyer Discipline*. He also is a member of the Board of Contributors of *Texas Lawyer* magazine. As a result of his work on this volume, he is researching a new book on humor malpractice.

Walter Richter, now semi-semi-retired, has served the public sector variously, as director of two state agencies and deputy commissioner of another — each of which survived his tenure — and director of a federal agency (regional), which survived him but not the Republican administration. His political life, all in the Democratic Party, includes service in the Texas Senate, two terms as Chair of the Travis County Democratic Party, and 10 years as a professional lobbyist. He is also a part-time rancher and free-lance writer.

If you have stories you would like to contribute to a future book on Texas political humor here's what to do. Please write out each story, joke, or other political humor item that you desire to contribute. It would be helpful if you could include any explanation that is useful or further identification of where and from whom you first heard the story, etc. There is no limit on the number of items that you may contribute. Please include your name, address, and telephone number and mail to Texas Political Humor, 301 Congress, Suite 1200, Austin, Texas 78701.